MW01127544

EARLY WORK

EARLY WORK

1970 – 1979

PATTI SMITH

W. W. NORTON & COMPANY
NEW YORK / LONDON

The text of this book is composed in 9.5/14 Claren-
don Light with display set in Clarendon Light.
Composition and manufacturing by the Haddon
Craftsmen, Inc.

BOOK DESIGN BY CHRIS WELCH

Library of Congress Cataloging-in-Publication Data
Smith, Patti.
    [Poems. Selections]
    Early work, 1970–1979 / Patti Smith.
        p.   cm.
    I. Title.
    PS3569.M53787A6   1994
    811'.54–dc20   93-23898

ISBN 0-393-03613-8 (limited edition)
ISBN 0-393-03605-7

W.W. Norton & Company, Inc., 500 Fifth Avenue
New York, N.Y. 10110

W.W. Norton & Company Ltd., 10 Coptic Street
London WC1A 1PU

    2 3 4 5 6 7 8 9 0

contents

Contents |

to the reader

All of the works gathered for this volume were
written in the seventies. In a time when the
passing of so many events, great and small,
spread an illuminating shadow across our path.
A long moody hand directing the motion of one
decade into another. Littering our way with
images—pressing our hearts and the bottom of
our shoes.

Time bleeding into time. Which we assaulted—
blurring and expanding the perimeters of love,
consciousness and remorse. Driven with the
collective hope to raise aspects of art, poetry,
rock n' roll, even charity that had not been
raised before.

A time, simply, when all my friends were alive.
Rats . . . wildboys . . . tramps in Victorian dress
Pirate-saints hovering the booty
The spoils of our predecessors
Pandora's box
where good and evil coupled so lovingly
greeting us, as an entity, so gaily clad
we perceived no ill grace

and so released
in the name of freedom, future
fragrances, fruit
our delight
and our price.

Upon a screen scenes stills go rushing by.
The changing truth of youth's uniform.
Youth untested, unbridled. Our hustling smiles.
Our lively limbs. We were as innocent and
dangerous as children racing cross a mine field.
Some never made it. Some drew the lot of more
treacherous fields. And some it seems turned out
all right and have lived to remember and salute
the others.

An artist wears his work in place of wounds.
Here then is a glimpse of the sores of my
generation. Often crude, irreverent—but done,
I can assure, with a fierce heart.

And so is offered in these optimistic tho
viral times a souvenir of another time
with this added prayer . . .

In art and dream may you proceed with abandon.
In life may you proceed with balance and stealth.

The seventies. When I think of them now I think
of one great film in which I played a part. A
bit part. But a part nonetheless that I shall
never play again.

to my mother and father

who weathered all

with resilience

humor and grace

1970–1972

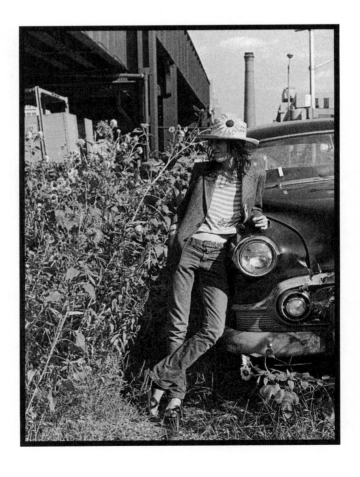

prayer

stocking feet or barefoot
immensely proud or bent like love
twig scaffold
grave digger or dancer in wind
the same wind yet stinking of pigs
rose or the pollen which makes one cough
cruel fantastic unlike anything else

to have no need for the apparatus
of the operating room
to be safe from all bodily harm
to know love without exception
to be a saint in any form

ballad of a bad boy

Oh I was bad
didn't do what I should
mama catch me with a lickin'
and tell me to be good
when I was bad twice times
she shoved me in a hole
and cut off all my fingers
and laid them in a finger bowl
my mama killed me
my papa grieved for me
my little sister Annalea
wept under the almond tree

Oh I loved a car
and when I was feelin' sad
I lay down on my daddy's Ford
and I'd feel good
and you know that I got bad
robbed hubcaps from the men
and sold them to the women
and stole them back again
and I got me a car
a Hudson Hornet car
and rolled the pretty ladies
and often went too far
I went to Chicago
I went to Kalamazoo
I went to Nashville
the highways I flew
I went to Salinas
I rode to the sea

and the people all scolded
and pointed to me
they said there's a bad boy
I was so bad boy
they gathered their daughters
I heard what they said
steer away from him, honey
'cause that boy is bad
and tho' he's hung good
and flashes that loot
don't slide by his side
he rides a wrong route
'cause he's a bad boy
I was so bad boy
my mama killed me
my papa grieved for me
my little sister Annalea
wept under the almond tree

And I wept on a stock car
I captured the junkyards
and I sped thru the canyons
though I never went far
from the wreckers mechanics
I worshiped these men
but they laughed at me, man
they called me mama's boy
mama mama mama mama . . .
Monday at midnight
Tuesday at two
drunk on tequila
thinking of you, ma
I drove my car on, ma
wrecking cars was my art

I held a picture of you, ma
close to my heart
I rode closed windows
it was ninety degrees
the crowd it was screaming
it was screaming for me
they said I was nonsense
true diver chicken driver
no sense
but I couldn't hear them
I couldn't see
fenders hot as angels
blazed inside of me
I sped on raged in steam heat
I cracked up and rolled at your feet
I rose in flames and rolled in a pit
where you caught me with a tire iron
and covered me in shit
and I coulda got up
but the crowd it screamed no
that boy is evil
too bad for parole
so bad his ma cut off all his fingers
and laid 'em in a finger bowl
his mama killed him
his papa grieved for him
his little sister Annalea
wept under the almond tree

Oh I was bad
didn't do what I should
mama catch me with a lickin'
and she tell me
You be good

oath

Jesus died for somebody's sins
but not mine
melting in a pot of thieves
wild card up my sleeve
thick heart of stone
my sins my own
I engrave my own palm
sweet black X
Adam placed no hex on me
I embrace Eve
and take full responsibility
for every pocket I have picked
mean and slick
every Johnny Ace song
I've balled to
long before the church
made it neat and right
So Christ
I'm giving you the good-bye
firing you tonight
I can make my own light shine
and darkness too is equally fine
you got strung up for my brother
but with me I draw the line
you died for somebody's sins
but not mine

anna of the harbor

anna of the harbor
anna full of grace
wrestles the desire
for the dwelling place
of male against male
where thieves gesticulate
and wink handsome
for the sailor lads
with duffle bags
stuffed with lace
Anna embroiders hopes
for marvelous tattoo rump
and sinks in perfumed
dressing gown
as blue-eyed beauties dance
but the men don't come
for anna of the harbor

anna full of grace
gazing from her favorite place
by the window
by the sea
by the thieves diaryed streets
where men wound and love
and make frank gestures
behind beaded curtains
as beads of sweat
drip and drip down
like a rosary
from unshaven pits
sliding velvet arms

holy ammonia waters
rising like old loves
rushing satin skirts
and anna of the harbor
with an automatic
feminine gesture
powders her dress
swift and expert
where her pantaloons
part like a woman

the sheep lady from algiers

nodding tho' the lamps lit low
nodding for passers underground
to and fro she's darning and
the yarn is weeping red and pale
marking the train stops from algiers

sleeping tho' the eyes are pale
hums in rhythum w/a bonnet on
lullaby a broken song
the sifting-cloth is bleeding red
weeping yarn from algiers

lullaby tho' baby's gone
the cradle rocks a barren song
she's rocking w/her ribbons on
she's rocking yarn and needles oh
it's long coming from algiers

work song

I was working real hard
to show the world
what I could do
oh I guess
I never dreamed
I'd have to
world spins
some photographs
how I love to laugh
when the crowd laughs
while love slips thru
a theater that is full
but ohh baby
when the crowd
when the crowd goes home
and I turn in
and I realize I'm alone
I can't believe
I can't believe
I had to
I was working real hard
to show the world
what I could do
oh I guess
I never dreamed
I'd have to
I had to
I had to
sacrifice
you

notebook

I keep trying to figure out what it means
to be american. When I look in myself
I see arabia, venus, nineteenth-century
french but I can't recognize what
makes me american. I think about
Robert Franks's photographs—broke down
jukeboxes in gallup, new mexico . . .
swaying hips and spurs . . . ponytails and
syphilitic cowpokes. I think about a
red, white and blue rag I wrap around
my pillow. Maybe it's nothing material
maybe it's just being free.

Freedom is a waterfall, is pacing
linoleum till dawn, is the right to
write the wrong words. and I done
plenty of that . . .

april 1971

conversation with the kid

who's the guy on the glass?
that's joyce.
joyce, that's a girl's name.
that's a name.
well, what's with him?
he watches over me.
he only got one eye.
a guy like him that's all he needs.

the ballad of hagen waker

(they say I have a circus soul. they call me
saint baalet. I have been walking ropes for them
for as long as I can remember.)

They call me saint baalet
due to my extraordinary balance
however don't be quick to judge
my trade is ruled by neurine
a poisonous ptomaine
my nerves are wired wired
and my middle ear is like a mouth
above ground I am miraculous angelic
so do not be alarmed by my appearance
I can boast a high birth
princess oxygen and gas
I waltz in a certain state of grace
and I am no common dancer
I have the eyes of a dancer
but I am no dancer
I am hagen waker
I'm a tightrope walker
And you sure look good to me.

As a high-wire artist
I am unique
every hall is stretched with silken braids
coated with phosphorus they glow in the dark
I am a night rope walker
I am billed higher than any performer
and dammit I live up to it
Consider the printed announcement

the testimony of the Circus Master:
   "Come see Saint Baalet
   the white velvet night walk
   she will perform her commune with toe air
   with a lizard lithe on either shoulder"
Oh. do not be alarmed by the birds either
I assure you they are but common european bats
but they look good in the act
they look good in the act
And you sure look good to me.

You know
it's often I'm glowing in the dark
dreaming of woman things
wishing I could get down to earth
But I've been mountain blind
for as long as I can remember.
That capricornous fever
of being higher than the crowd
as for the crowd
they are ecstatic
they hollar for more
and roar when I leave them
Often their cries merit several encores
"Stay on your toes, baalet," they cry.
And I whisper:
Don't breathe
don't shout
my slippers are ribboned
don't breathe on my feet
and they hold it
hold it
for hours and hours
till their face turns blue

(and hagen waker seems nights away
  and I'd like to leave
  but I stay and stay)
I swallow radium pills
So I shine in the dark
So I'm filled with power
when the lights blow out
But won't you be patient till the show is over
Oh Billy Dancer I need a good lover
And you sure look good to me.

Christ you know the moon is full tonight
I'd like to run out wringing wet
and shake my hair loose under it
instead my nights stretch beneath this tent
balance balance I got to keep
my wits and invent new tricks
to knock them dead
I am a tightrope walker
trapped in a carnival
they will never let me go. no.
I have a long-term bond. oh
balance balance I got to keep
and should you pass while I'm rehearsing
please don't startle me
I'm not one to use a net
I might fall for you
I might give it all to you
and the crowds would bleed
I've been theirs for as long as I can remember
but christ when the moon is full
I'd like to get the hell out of here
Step light like their angel
then shimmy like evil

And you sure look good to me.

And you know I'm willing to come down for you
after hours when the show is through
when I'm more down to earth
and the crowd has gone home
(I will admit the show lasts forever)
But I have this nervous gesture
that they like and leap for
for that alone I can not leave them
with the dancing monkey in a pinstripe shirt
with the donkey-faced boy
making an ass of himself
with sexy Laurello with the revolving head
with the reptile woman shedding crocodile tears
The crowd won't fall for them
So I gotta give it all to them
They abuse every act in the tent
Save my circus soul
and lose interest in the show
when I have to go
but wait for me, Billy Dancer
won't you, Billy Dancer
I get the blues like any good woman
I want to come down and be used
like any good woman
long after I've showed my nerve to the crowd
A dish of something good is certainly allowed
after the rope
the next step is to fly
And I sure would like
some of your custard pie
I sure would like some of your custard pie
I sure would like some of your custard pie

seventh heaven

Oh Raphael. Guardian angel. In love and crime
all things move in sevens. seven compartments
in the heart. the seven elaborate temptations.
seven devils cast from Mary Magdalene whore
of Christ. the seven marvelous voyages of Sinbad.
sin/bad. And the number seven branded forever
on the forehead of Cain. The first inspired man.
The father of desire and murder. But his was not
the first ecstasy. Consider his mother.

Eve's was the crime of curiosity. As the saying
goes: it killed the pussy. One bad apple spoiled
the whole shot. But be sure it was no apple.
An apple looks like an ass. It's fags' fruit.
It must have been a tomato.
Or better yet. A mango.
She bit. Must we blame her. abuse her.
poor sweet bitch. perhaps there's more to the story.
think of Satan as some stud.
maybe her knees were open.
satan snakes between them.
they open wider
snakes up her thighs
rubs against her for a while
more than the tree of knowledge was about
to be eaten . . . she shudders her first shudder
pleasure pleasure garden
was she sorry
are we ever girls
was she a good lay
god only knows

amelia earhart

amelia earhart
earheart
ear
heart
air

amelia earhart. dupe. first lady of the skies.
she had no guy holding her down.
no one could clip her wings.
she was no bird in the hand.
she is no living thing now.
she is ageless. parachute.
they never got her. not her.
she cut out clean blue.
it was all there.
one afternoon I was polishing off still another
hand of cards. they said deal straight. crazy eight.
yer not playing with a full deck.
yer looking red around the eyes.
it was true. yet I wasnt nodding.
I was hearing that music.
ancient aeroplane.

now I got rights to those words. it was all
there I tell ya. out the window. after moon.
etched in sky.
writing
she said:

my step is heavy
but i can fly like an angel
and so like a hawk am i now
my elbows flap like wings.

k.o.d.a.k.
plea to george franju

picture this. I'll play the killer. 16 millimeter.
ebony and ivory. the purest contrast. iris closed.
open sesame. a screen of creamy white satin.
on that wedding lap a white persian cat. a pale
hand pets. milk purr. pan up slow. it's me see.
in a black silk suit. dark glasses. kid gloves.
as sinister as the law allows. I've returned
from the opera. prowl cat tom cat.
if I'm male it doesn't matter.

I'm on the ledge. that's a several story drop.
how did I execute my brilliant cat walk? that's
up to you, franju. but there I am. perched on her
window sill like a dirty bluebird. the back of my
neck is wet. I sit there what seems for hours.
a human chess game. she makes the first move.

it's quite simple. she gets up to adjust her
sloppy stocking. her easter spikes could use
some vaseline. her matt gesture is reflected
in black patent leather. shoot to the ruffled
vanity. mirror image. look at the kisser
gazing from that mica. lipstick so thick
you could carve your initials in it.

no alias not me. my initials are PLS and I'd be
pleased to leave my monogram. close-up shot
of my steady fist. I'm cool as menthol. the kind
of confidence one achieves thru an open nose.

cocaine. I can do it. watch me raise my leather
fingers. bluebeard itching for a fleshy white neck.
I strike. she's no match for me. the cold adhesive
touch of the octopus. I remove my glove.
struggle struggle. glub glub. she's gone.

as the opening credits roll up. the killer,
swift as an athlete, is escaping.
springing from roof top to roof top.
racing against pyramid shapes
into the black seine.

search party music. the killer.
16 mm. black and white.
g. franju. with patti smith.

george franju. media me.
shoot me on the kodak.
I'll do it for free.

dog dream

have you seen
dylan's dog
it got wings
it can fly
if you speak
of it to him

its the only
time dylan
can't look you in the eye

have you held
dylan's snake
it rattles like a toy
it sleeps in the grass
it coils in his hand
it hums and it strikes out
when dylan cries out
when dylan cries out

have you pressed
to your face
dylan's bird
dylan's bird
it lies on dylan's hip
trembles inside of him
it drops upon the ground
it rolls with dylan round
it's the only one
who comes
when dylan comes

have you seen
dylan's dog
it got wings
it can fly
when it lands
like a clown
he's the only
thing allowed
to look dylan in the eye

jeanne d'arc

I feel like
I feel like shit
I need a
I need a drink
and not vinegar neither
I don't want to die
I feel like a freak
don't let me cut out
I wasn't cut out
to go out virgin
I want my cherry
squashed man
hammer amour
love me
live me
hour to death
what the hell
hour to death
am I doing here
am I ending here
hour of death
and I feel so free
feel like fucking
feel so free
feel like running
got no hair
weighing me
cut so close
scalp is nicked
look like shit
hour of darkness

and I look like shit
hour to death and I feel so free
hour to death and I feel so free
turnkey turnkey
play with my pussy
lick my little
scull bait head
get it get it
get it in
get the guard to
beg the guard to
need a guard to
lay me
get all the guards to lay me
if all the guards would lay me
if one guard would lay me
if one guard would lay me
if one god would lay me
if one
god

a fire of unknown origin

you're displeased
maybe I should just stop
being you

A fire of unknown origin
took my baby away
a fire of unknown origin
took my baby away
swept her up and off
my wave length
swallowed her up like the ocean
in a fire thick and gray

death comes sweeping
thru the hallway
like a ladies dress
death comes riding
down the highway
in its sunday best

death comes driving
death comes creeping
death comes
I can't do nothing
death goes
there must be something
that remains
death it made me sick and crazy
'cause that fire
it took my baby
away

she left me everything
she left me all her things

death by water

How long ago was man promised?
never again. no not again.
no death by water.

yet how many questions arise like yeast.
like the perfect dead:

was the red sea really?
does man rule the river?
did she/he drown?
was it natural causes?
was it sorrow?

How many tears on your pillow.
crocodile or real. water shed.
brian jones drowned. face down.
in a child's pool of water. youth fountain.

Jim Morrison. our leather lamb. he feared
the bathroom. he warned us. hyacinth house.
how did he know. how did christ know. no
doubt about it. a marked man is always the
first to know. he died in a bathtub. slumped
over like Marat. the only clue was the red
rash over his heart.
someone said there were last words. water
poured from his eyes. he was truly immaculate
yet surprised. outside it was raining. storm
clouds. danger waters. the tub was overflowing.
he looked up. then he cried out:
"but you promised"

the amazing tale of skunkdog

*don't be surprised if death
comes from within . . .*

seven days and six nights the hero watched relent-
lessly. horizontally under the sky. without food,
drink or friend. what was he after. what was he look-
ing for. a sign? an answer? a way out? something
new.

now on the seventh evening of the seventh day hero
was holding on by a thread. lack of sleep, provisions
and loving arms was taking its toll. he ceased to look
up.

fair hero. he who was so intent on keeping his eyes
peeled immediately missed out.

for hero had made the sky jumpy. his piercing
stares put it on edge. when he finally looked down
the stars went haywire. cassiopeia rocked like a
cradle.

any chance observer unable to sleep. dreaming out a
window. counting sheep. would not have believed
his eyes. the milky way shook out shook out. a flock
of shooting stars. random comets. and the great dog
star so there like a new born moon. yet hero saw
nothing.

see a watched sky is like a watched pot. the minute
hero gave up the heavens boiled over. meteorites and

planet action passed over him like any common bat.
what could he say. he was in a mean condition. his
tongue was getting fuzzy to say nothing of his vi-
sion. his eyes were seeing double of nothing.

was all lost? not on his life. it looked bad. but see it
this way: hero was finally getting down to earth.

suddenly (as in any monumental movie)
there occured a chain of events
that pierced his very being; his very soul.
giving all formal experience the old heave-ho:
seven red ants bit his left hand
six smooth stones rolled from his tongue
his five fingers stretched an octave
four yellow feathers appeared from nowhere
as did three blue birds
over his head (halo) circled two luna moths
he was hungry so he snapped like the iguana
two moths were eaten.
his stomach fluttered
he was numb black out
sleep overcame him
(for one minute only
tho' it seemed like hours)
and he dreamed this dream:

HOPE HE IS IN NO DANGER

he is led to the spawning ground of certain
sacred animals. he fears he will be forced to
copulate with one. native dancers circle him
then close in. they strip him down. his birthday
suit has changed clothes. he has a new feminine

figure. they cleanse him. they polish his body
with ox-blood oil. he is instructed to choose an
animal.

a striped tom brushes his leg. a gray and gold tom
with big blue eyes. eyes so blue hero's mouth waters.
a slick skinned cow with lacquer red udders (very
chinese) stretches and rolls in a mound of cornflow-
ers. blue flowers. bluer than the cat's eye.

hero wonders about his own eyes. in this atmo-
sphere do they also appear bluer than they really
are? damn not a mirror in sight. will the effect wear
off when he returns home? he hopes not.

to his left are the green green hills. a cold menthol
green. he glances over and gasps. he sees skunkdog.
it is a huge mastiff with long shining hair. black
hair. his joint, unlike most dogs with their slimy
rouge pistols, is pure white. hero throbs down there
like a woman and cannot resist making an obscene
gesture.

skunkdog opens his eyes wide. two huge blue sau-
cers. the bluest eyes imaginable. bluer than the corn-
flowers. bluer than the mediterranean sea.

hero is overcome. wanton. he turns away then looks
back. oh no! skunkdog is gone. hero races across to
the green hills. he is naked and children are laugh-
ing. he could care less. he uproots trees, plants and
boulders. he pulls his hair out by the roots. every-
where strange animals are mating. steam is rising.
women are eating whale meat. other women are ex-
posing their bellies.

down a gully he spies skunkdog. he's been skinned.
there is his fresh carcass. hero falls prostrate. gets
set to grieve. when, out of the blue, he is brought
the skin of his slain beloved.
he slips it on.
it's a perfect fit.
he is no longer hero.
he is no long hero
but black-haired blue-eyed

SKUNK DOG!

doggod dog/god doggod
the dog jumps over the moon.

1973–1974

notice

These ravings, observations, etc. come from one who, beyond vows, is without mother, gender, or country. who attempts to bleed from the word a system, a space base. no rock island but a body of phrases with all the promise of top soil or a star. a core: a center that will hold, blossom and vein the atmosphere with vascular tissue beams that illuminate and reveal.

longing for . . . a ticket. a slit. a peephole. some sign from—. holding to the naïve belief that travel will open—. get physically sick like adolescent. no hand-job for the word save travel. save one devour manual, route map and dictionaire. save ritual. save rhythm. save cous cous. godhead dialect? foreign tongue kiss? internal voyage: brain rocket. god my skull. yes travel is the key, not, as rimbaud suggested, charity.

wĭtt

i

where there were angels I saw no one. nothing. not even space. the air an ice milk. banana popsicle. white paper. time stretching like a hand that covers. gotta beat time. got a longing, for the great departure. travel. search party. safari. distant places. dialects, jungles, pagodas. desert love nest.

ii

look at this land where we am. lost souls. failed moon over the carnival. deserted. there is no twilight on this island. night falls like a final curtain. how shakespearean. carnival of fools. of the seduced and the discarded. the tricked ones. the skinned ethiopian. sleeping thru the whole thing. the leopard rolling over. all but blushing with the discovery of his sleek coat sans spot.

iii

pass out the mustard seed. slide one under the tongue. encase in crystal. wrap in the leaves of a bible. I'm dead tired. slit mine in half. slip part one 'neath my fingernail. owwww yell what torture. at least I'll remember. walking in the sand. stranger. chloroform . . .

iv

I am experiencing courtship with the angels. instead of caresses they beat their pure feathers. rapid

wing move. vain-o-bleach peacock. more incredible
than the prized chinese fans. fans that plucked the
white heron dry and bald. they beat beat. they leave
me breathless. undefiled yet satisfied. completely
wiped out. still I wonder . . . is it possible there is yet
a more natural light. one that rips and zings. highly
polished fat chrome arrow.

v

see me walk thru the jungle. naked how noble. the
only surviving savage. civilized yet without a stitch.
overhead is the white eagle. huge mythic. be he al-
bino or mystic it's the same to me. he's big as a hut
now. his cock comes down. like a ladder from the
belly of the helicopter rescue. immense perfect lad-
der. monkey bridge. an arc. a runway. so inview that
I can see the animals run up by twos. to shelter
safety he's upon me. we know what to do. to move
the night with love. synchronization of breath. sex,
unlike the stranger, can move mountains. and me
I'm one gaping hole. a cock pit. and his (the eagle's)
is so fitting. doth me protest. for a second, no-ahhh.
virtue expendable. angels blotted

where there were no spiders I saw spiders
penetration till it comes like the flood.

piss factory

Sixteen and time to pay off I got this job in a piss factory inspecting pipe Forty hours thirty-six dollars a week but it's a paycheck, jack. It's so hot in here hot like sahara You could faint in the heat but these bitches are just too lame to understand too goddamn grateful to get this job to know they're getting screwed up the ass.

All these women they got no teeth or gum in cranium And the way they suck hot sausage but me well I wasn't sayin' too much neither I was moral school girl hard-working asshole I figured I was speedo motorcycle had to earn my dough had to earn my dough.

But no you gotta relate, right, you gotta find the rhythm within. Floor boss slides up to me and he says "Hey sister, you just movin' too fast. You screwin' up the quota. You doin' your piece work too fast. Now you get off your mustang sally, you ain't goin' nowhere, you ain't goin' nowhere."

I lay back. I get my nerve up. I take a swig of romilar and walk up to hot shit Dot Hook and I say "Hey, hey sister, it don't matter whether I do labor fast or slow, there's always more labor after." She's real Catholic, see. She fingers her cross and she says "There's one reason. There's one reason. You do it my way or I push your face in. We knee you in the john if you don't get off your mustang, Sally, if you don't shake it up baby." Shake it up baby. Twist and shout.

Oh that I could will a radio here. James Brown singing I lost someone. Oh the Paragons and the Jesters and Georgie Woods the guy with the goods and

Guided Missles . . . but no, I got nothin', no diversion no window nothing here but a porthole in the plaster where I look down at sweet Theresa's convent all those nuns scattin' 'round with their bloom hoods like cats in mourning. oh to me they look pretty damn free down there not having to smooth those hands against hot steel not having to worry about the inspeed the dogma the inspeed of labor. oh they look pretty damn free down there and the way they smell and here I gotta be up here smellin' Dot Hook's midwife sweat.

I would rather smell the way boys smell—oh those schoolboys the way their legs flap under the desk in study hall that odor rising roses and ammonia and the way their dicks droop like lilacs. Or the way they smell that forbidden acrid smell. But no I got pink clammy lady in my nostril. Her against the wheel me against the wheel Oh slow motion inspection is drivin' me insane in steel next to Dot Hook—oh we may look the same—shoulder to shoulder sweatin' hundred and ten degrees But I will never faint. They laugh and they expect me to faint but I will never faint I refuse to lose refuse to fall down because you see it's the monotony that's got to me every after-noon like the last one every afternoon like a rerun next to Dot Hook and yeah we look the same both pumpin' steel both sweatin'.

But you know she got nothin' to hide and I got some-thing to hide here called desire I got something to hide here called desire. And I will get out of here—you know the fiery potion is just about to come. In my nose is the taste of sugar and I got nothin' to hide here save desire And I'm gonna go I'm gonna get out of here I'm gonna get on that train and go to New

York City and I'm gonna be somebody I'm gonna get
on that train and go to New York City and I'm gonna
be so bad, I'm gonna be a big star and I will never
return never return no never return to burn out in
this Piss factory.
And I will travel light.
Oh watch me now.

recorded at Electric Ladyland

June 5, 1974

balance

Born to be. born to be me. just the right
dark glasses.
the power of the image. treat
the cornea like a jewel.
sapphire seurat dot.
pull vision in. inverted flashlight.

and out. zero out before it's too late. parachute.
like the berber nomad. never stick around
for more then.
not a sign of. instamatic
travelogue.
the hungry eye.

continual movement. via fiat. on foot. the great
club footed canal. in the congo. whistle rimbaud.
witness the angry aim of insane birds. offset.
crush their micro-blue helmets. metabolic cobalt.

paint my naked frame matisse style. a stylistic
trick. a breathing portrait. sacred leopard.
shed my genet-skin. gotta run. I'm a surface
skimmer. iceskate. skull cap. perhaps the sky.
if it be the true canopy. build the great
trampoline. I'll attempt the big bounce.

Bong. it can be done. olympic formula? language
à la McClure. the intricate balance of belmondo.
the confused grace of buster keaton. the optic
movement of anna karina a wisp of silk.
pole star. a chance must not be missed.
jump that compass fever gun.
a risk is just a risk.

dream of rimbaud

I am a widow. could be charleville could be any-
where. move behind the plow. the fields. young ar-
thur lurks about the farmhouse (roche?) the pump
the artesian well. throws green glass alias crystal
broken. gets me in the eye.

I am upstairs. in the bedroom bandaging my wound.
he enters. leans against the four-poster. his ruddy
cheeks. contemptuous air big hands. I find him sexy
as hell. how did this happen he asks casually. too
casually. I lift the bandage. reveal my eye a bloodied
mess; a dream of Poe. he gasps.

I deliver it hard and fast. someone did it. you did it.
he falls prostrate. he weeps he clasps my knees. I
grab his hair. it all but burns my fingers. thick fox
fire. soft yellow hair. yet that unmistakable red
tinge. rubedo. red dazzle. hair of the One.

Oh jesus I desire him. filthy son of a bitch. he licks
my hand. I sober. leave quickly your mother waits.
he rises. he's leaving. but not without the glance,
from those cold blue eyes, that shatters. he who hesi-
tates is mine. we're on the bed. I have a knife to his
smooth throat. I let it drop. we embrace. I devour his
scalp. lice fat as baby thumbs. lice the skull's caviar.

Oh arthur arthur. we are in Abyssinia Aden. mak-
ing love smoking cigarettes. we kiss. but it's much
more. azure. blue pool. oil slick lake. sensations tele-
scope, animate. crystalline gulf. balls of colored
glass exploding. seam of berber tent splitting. open-
ings, open as a cave, open wider. total surrender.

notice 2

joke: *once, if I remember well, I sat judy on my knees and . . .*

how, when all else failed: bird, magician, desert mirage, the prospect of gold and riches beyond the cloak and sleeve of marco polo, I attached all to an image—a muse amused.

caught like a squirrel on high tension wire. an image worthy of worship of monastery. with every vice divine. no morals required etc. this love, at first glance, a concrete and very fertile egg. later to be cracked and revealed as colossal pride. as there and as fruitless as the parthenon (sans goddess). the tourists' postcard. the illusion of grandeur.

picking over the ruins of this romance this comedy like hungry prehistoric. slender minarets, white and crumbling like sugar teeth. song (this moment) on the radio: as I walk this land of broken dreams.

blushing monument: pink sphinx. sizzling squirrel. fallen pharaoh. the exhaustion of the mind which attempts to penetrate the mystery of. . . .

judith revisited (fragments)
the ladies room is ravaged

i

your tribe. white car. a whole spectrum of whites. whiter than the knight. her matinee pearls. the dress shirt of judex. the magician's glove. whiter still than the dove in the hand

holy ghost? no baby this is no symbol this is for real. crystallized vapor cold powder. snort that cerebral stuff. put your tongue in my mouth. speed and slow motion. inner search light. or have I been robbed? jack-off in the bathroom. perfect snow job

electric brain-o. hairy halo. itchy claroil. me I blond now. admire mirror what is paler? linen napkin. coconut chiffon curtain. the bridal bed. mother milk. wrinkled sheet. extraction of teeth. immense ivory. bash my brains out. egyptian maggot

ii

sudan the royal secret. mining and extraction guarded. ivory cone. cone gun. mujah. juju extracting my teeth and bleach tonsils. atom ideas alkimia blood love between us serve purpose. allow me to relax as well as give her confidence. amateur operation with handful of small tools. novocaine administered with miniature hypodermic
only lips move. love poem call silk root.
ruined roman/anna magnani/rose
over tokyo/ lick a cultured pearl

iii

I'm ancient I'm stunning I'm just your style. your seed your private dilemma. my dentist hogwash. there's spit on my teeth. aren't you afraid they'll find out about us. how we hump it up in the outhouse. do you burn my letters confess. or are they locked in a closet in some rolltop desk medicine chest strong box poste box anywhere with a kee-ee. no worry I'll sleuth them out every envelope. me I detective. a very private dick. sniff sniff beagle brain. your bush needs clipping. your mouth needs kissing. dog kiss. tu-lips. in the open mouth of your corvette.

honey feel so crazy. not stylishly. not brilliant. just so I can't remember the last sentence. what I was looking for. the moment before. daydream has no plot characters just words. strung together. no not loosely. you aren't listening. tight dense just like tom thumb rhino choker. correction: pearl choker.

iv

juju, what are you writing? a party invitation. only lips move. my upper lip is frost bit. puffy a blond ubangi. bite me a little. bite me a lock of your hair. bite me a hot dog. no give me a bite to eat. what you write?

you draw palm tree/ I drink pepsi
I want to be a landscape painter.

oh that's good. that's very good. we go to red sea. you paint a pyramid you paint your toes red. and me I stay in bed. I hold my head. freeze all that is said. only words move.

v

oh jesus write it out of your body baby wait wait all
night. weary day. is snow too romantic? we could do
it in the snow. washing your hair. bending over the
tub. running my soapy forefinger down your spine.
you on your knees bent over the tub. your breasts
out of shape swaying like two golden bells. I'm the
gardener you're lady chatterly. I stand up. turn
around and suck my dick.

washing your hair. maybe too romantic. so what
clock. I imagine you on the nile. that neck of yours
enough to make Nefertiti blush. the delicious white
slump of your shoulder after

love it wears off. there's grass stains on your dress.
we are nearly finished. a cold july with her. in her
sunsuit. her fleshy legs. when I press my thumb
against it makes a white mark. the powder on her
wrist. her ballet scar. all things pure.

human? no mam. mistress is gelatin. atom.

she's a football player. one night. no it's dusk. in
back of the bleachers. blondest sweetest football vir-
gin. hardon softest leather buttocks. lick it up her
delicious teen-age sweat. show her how. make her
again. leave her dazed confused exhausted defiled
spidered black as coal. oooy-gooey all over her high
school letter. kick her in the side. in the ear. words
pour

I leave you lying there. I am intact. and I don't care.
(rimbaud)

georgia o'keeffe

great lady painter
what she do now
she goes out with a stick
and kills snakes

georgia o'keeffe
all life still
cow skull
bull skull
no bull shit
pyrite pyrite
she's no fool
started out pretty
pretty pretty girl

georgia o'keeffe
until she had her fill
painted desert
flower cactus
hawk and head mule
choral water color
red coral reef
been around forever
georgia o'keeffe

great lady painter
what she do now
go and beat the desert
stir dust bowl
go and beat the desert
snake skin skull
go and beat the desert
all life still

picasso laughing

notebook
divine love is so.
invisible.

notebook
november 1. all souls day. rimbaud-o. go
to hell. picasso knows. how he really fucking
knew knows. where can he go now.

notebook
picasso hoax: don't nobody tell when he dies.
continue let time continue and move like myth.
till suddenly somebody rings a bell. says over
a dinner party why he he is over a century.
or more perfect two centuries.

diary. sunday. april 8, 1973.
picasso dies

april is the cruelest month etc. what remains?
brian jones bones. jim morrison's friend.
jimi hendrix bandana. sweatband angel.
the starched collar of baudelaire.
the sculptured cap of voltaire.
the crusader's helmet like a temple itself
carole lombard's handmirror.
brancusi bird brain.
the prodigal kiss.
judies garland. rimbaud's valise.
rothko's overcoat. surreal space.
the black knit dress of piaf.

photographs. picasso laughing. picasso dancing.
picasso do the fishback. picasso do the cadillac.
a heartbreak a brushstroke. the light streaming
the window of the villa. sun rising and setting
and sleeping on clean white sheets all folded
and picasso's boatneck shirt.

rape

yum yum the stars are out. I'll never forget how you smelled that night. like cheddar cheese melting under fluorescent light. like a day-old rainbow fish. what a dish. gotta lick my lips. gotta dream I daydream. thorozine brain cloud. rain rain comes coming down.

all over her. there she is on the hill. pale as a posy. getting soaking wet. hope her petticoats shrink. well little shepherd girl your gonna kingdom come. looking so clean. the guardian of every little lamb. well beep beep sheep I'm moving in.

I'm gonna peep in bo's bodice. lay down darling don't be modest let me slip my hand in. ohhh that's soft that's nice that's not used up. ohhh don't cry. wet what's wet? oh that. heh heh. that's just the rain lambie pie. now don't squirm. let me put my rubber on. I'm a wolf in a lamb skin trojan. ohh yeah that's hard that's good. now don't tighten up. open up be-bop. lift that little butt up. ummm open wider be-bop. come on. nothing. can. stop me. now. ohhh ahhh. isn't that good. my. melancholy be-bop.

Oh don't cry. come on get up. let's dance in the grass. let's cut a rug let's jitterbug. roll those tiny white stockings down. bobby sock-o let's flow. come on this is a dance contest. under the stars, let's alice in the grass.

let's swing betty boop hoop
let's birdland let's stroll
let's rock let's roll
let's whalebone let's go
let's deodorize the night.

gibralto

i

Babies insurance. I dont love nobody. that's my pol-
icy. least of all Gibralto. the swine. he walked out on
me. picked up his hard butt and walled me up here.
and when I'm alone any four walls close in on me.
ballroom bathroom any room at all. ceilings pull
down. yeah ceilings. I've looked up at plenty under
him. is he really gone? am I really alone? am I good
for nothing?
I can't keep my mind on anything. I keep pacing
forth and back. timepiece. the smokes and nescafe is
all that keeps me intact. who invented the hot plate?
rare genius. compact. mine is constantly fired. pass
me that deck of kools. ah menthol. another refresh-
ing invention. oh that's good, with nescafe thick as
sauce in my gut and a butt hanging from my lip I
feel whole again.

ii

dishes crank on my nerves

iii

Well I'm pissed and when I'm pissed I'm up for any-
thing. I'll get his ugly mug out of my system. I'll
draw his face down. that will fix him. he keeps his
soul clean. camera shy bastard. but I'll capture him.
I'm artistic see. as cold-eyed as the national geo-
graphic. shall I make his physique classic. shall I

make him colorful. that's a laugh. what color is a
crawling louse?
I'll draw me in to. beautiful dreamers. I'll make them
tongue kiss. ahh now they're hot. the pencil jig-
gles. they ball. together. oh man. I can't draw it
down. I'm no draftsman. I'm no fucking draftsman.
and my cast eye escapes perspective. eye. I. baby I
got my one blue eye on you. you're my devils food
cake. CRACK.

iv

get me emergency. I've fucked my fist on my shiny
new cupboard. he's real romantic see. he gets me a
cupboard see. he says look toots it's cleverly de-
signed. everything fits except the kitchen sink. put
a little order in yer life.
put a little blood on my knuckle.
a few splinters in my fist.
my cups falleth to the floor.

v

I wanna crack somebody good. ya need to feel some-
body's face under yer fist. knuckles get yellow.
shaky yellow fist. so pissed. feel to kill. if nothing
just to kill time. time the betrayer. my timex ticks
slow motion.

you ask for love you get horseshit. you get too much
you don't get any. sooner or later everyone takes a
rap in this racket. this racket called love. my num-
bers come up. you can bet if you're a loser.

long long hours pacing the floor. call myself every name in the book and a few extra. excuse me while I tear myself to pieces. must be someway I can repay that bastard. I killed a roach as big as my hand. my fucking hand is killing me.

vi

christ. the crap you write when somebody gives you the sack. sick of faking it. want to settle down. with him. have bambinos wash his socks. its getting me down. trying. to pretend. oh baby I know you don't want to own me but why don't you come back anyway. baby get me out of the dark here baby I need you here. baby. eyeball failing. hardship.

vii

rhum
heart sick
heart shit
heart shit

hearts pounding. mad ticker. I write with excitement. I imagine it's you mounting the stairs.

viii

the ivory soap cleanses my sins.

ha! ha! houdini!

Harry Rouclere!!!

ever hear of him? an illuminated man. yet he traded
his magic light for the life of a flyer. tacked on his
wings and laid his cards on the table. you gotta hand
it to him. his heart was in the right place. he was
quite a man.

But Harry Houdini was more than a man.
he was an angel.

true. an imperfect one. he lacked the wings of a dove. but he had spirit. he kept trying.

now every great magician marvels ascension. that's why they're all fans of Christ. and our hero was no exception. Houdini proclaimed Christ the father of aviation. the absolute upper crust. the guy who writ every trick in the book and a few extra. who climbed the sky like a clean white airplane. without aid of propeller or parachute. who needed no ticket stamped TWA. perfectly hijack proof. who shook hands with the heavens long before the invasion of modern false flyers.

Q: was houdini a fraud?
A: was christ?

Harry is known in higher stations as the 13th apostle.

His name was fake but he was not. he was no alchemist. no scientist. no trickster plucking radishes from top hats. no cup and ball man. no heaven-born conjuror. but a man who sought heaven thru natural magic. he studied our savior's tactics religiously. he was internally airborne. and driven with such an obsessive desire to mount the sky he soon proved himself to be a tru-blue pilot.

yet his aerial triumphs are little known. he is still worshiped as the great escape artist. the supreme shackle cracker.

was ever there a man so misunderstood? Harry was
not merely escaping. he was on his way somewhere.

LOOK BACK:
Harry was born premature. he was hot as hell to get
out. yes, born in budapest. at the top of the world.
and before he was out of knee pants he ran off. to
join the circus. he ran fast. extending even the earli-
est dreams into movement.

Why, known even in pure youth for his uncanny
feats. and in later years ropes locks barrels jails nor
manacles could hold him down. nothing but nothing
could fence him in.

Men (and women too) had tried. from chicago to
moscow. from gangster to emperor.

one remembers him jogging the russian racetrack.
plotting his break, beat by beat, from their steel-
lined siberian prison van.

like jonah he popped from a giant german fish! a
whale of a tale. but it's true all true.

there were the open air straightjacket escapes that
made the entire south gasp.

he amazed the mighty Chinks by struggling from
their chinese water torture cell.

there were the dangerous underwater acts. when
failure meant a drowning death. yet he had no fear.

'Cause as its been said: he was not merely escaping.
he was shooting. for the stars maybe. he was testing.
how low he could go. thru and up and over.

aiming to pierce that gravity ceiling many call heaven.

his marvelous feats were but warm-ups for the big break.

Ah Houdini. he tried it. he didn't do it. he died before it. quick. but he died game.

And he'll be back he'll be back he'll be back . . .

One night when you least expect it. the moon will crack like an egg. and sliding down that long gold stream will be no easter chick . . .

It will be Houdini! Harry Houdini. with a wave a flourish and a smile that will break the heart of every locksmith in America.

schinden

and that night. the white electric storm. the lake
in flames. you sleeping so soundly. your big bones.
smooth forehead. your dry pale mouth. split lip skin
flakes. to bite them off with needlepoint precision
to chew and roll in a minute translucent ball
and spit ball against the horizon. skin. it's so
wonderful peeling your back after summer.
a perfect sheet of skin. pores backprint
and some blond down. your backbone fossil.
the sickly olive patch beneath

pressing the veil of skin against my face.
sucking some in with every breath.
sting rain the bay windows hypodermic.
in the skull the electric whirlwind.
sucking more with every breath.
skin erection all symbols of a bliss.
I was so amazed so moved I loved you so much.

16 february

Linda, your birthday was the worst one. I awoke with your name on my lips but the room was already tilting and spinning. noxema cold waving hot skin my hands two red paws radiating violet threads ribs peeling intestine shuddering room rising and swelling shit and disinfectant and pale vermin burrowing. One tender moment the fever lifts the overhead fan a white propeller shifts spraying shadow across whitewashed walls shells my left arm and I drift. A child holds on to a snowflake candles illuminate your trusting face. happy birthday my sister, syrupy hairs stick to my cheek purple spine merging plastic sheet. happy birthday sister, I reach relief my burnoose yards of cheesecloth cocoon to roll up in water a distant pitcher liquid streaming golden stars so aware of teeth and temples and the heat avenging moving in like squatter laughing with huge white teeth like tombstone and so aware of the temple on the hill surrounded by jackangels.

hotel internacional mexico
16.2.74

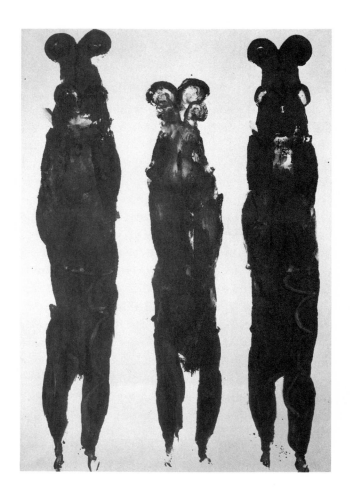

jet flakes

tender stranger. gentle stranger. why strangle
the rose. jewel. geometric sea. the hook rising
from the blank diamond. black facets revealing
the source of a space. and I who long to see so
much prop my lids with discarded sticks. with
eyes and lips dry as desert ships. from what

pool shall I drink. to what process shall I
submit. shall I bleat like a goat. shall I pray
for grain to spurt the motionless field. shall
I turn away having extracted no more than a
tooth from bone pale ash. black facets flake.
tender ache.

tender angel. turning angles. I lay before your
feet a branch of foolscap. how I long for it.
that which breeds in these heavy mounds. what
the earth erupts. pearl. lotus. knowledge in
general. to wear as a ring round my neck. a black
tube hard as cunning. a mica spool that I may sew
these threats. give me I desire it. I am no
breathless starlet but starchip. I fall whoosh
like meteorite but I do not burn out. I spew and
gush mercury silverhead. I spread my net. I
tarnish the grass.

I sink in the shadow of dust. the sakaara mi cara.
I am nothing but glass. if one should step upon my
surface brittle as it is I would shiver a thousand
pieces. each sliver betraying a desire.
to be as a sprinkle of gold from the mines of opfira.
to spin like a fish in the river quelle.
to be a lash of soot plucked from the pink eternal.
to be a face no stranger than yours.
with a conscience of wax
melting with midnight.

translators *(tr.)*

i

thank the stars for translators. the cream of the planet. I am completely useless. the thick air that surrounds me also holds me up. keep my hair slicked. seal skin skull cap. plaster brain mold. desire for . . . travel. taken on such force, gastric complications etc. malady rocks and slags. more than mildly parasitic. toughest albumin glue. like those pairs of magnetic scottie dogs one buys in vending machines. magnetized doggies rocking together. nearly falling away. always clinging siamese at the last moment.

the leaves of the african violet sweat beads. venetian finery. the pelican. the bambara. the dogon. oh know 2:49. some soul music. no music like soul music. god kiss marvin gaye trouble man. the miracle of motown. majorette precision. sing nigger sing sing.

hail. the night rain. how the sidewalks (wet) sprouted hair. grew very fast like florida wonderplant. long and waving. very much in the need of combing

how all words. written. american. see all words as amputees. no arms. arms akimbo. invisible arms dying to be seen. to wave out. spatial break. colloquial arabic

how site line stretched endless desert. there sat 30 arabs. in white dresses. they opened their mouths and started singing. algebraic muzak. first neon squares tumbled out. animated desert disney. gradually unraveling chant chant. vertical neon snaking across the sands. forming hills hump fountain dunes according to pitch tone etc. soon the arabs fell back. but the voice remained and traveled on. like loving arms embraced the earth. saturn arm bands. wandering star. perfect harmony. ha ha he he

ii

physical atomic end. ta-ta. ta-ta. tata tata caca. eat my shit id eat your shit ill eat your shit. tata. ta-ta gobi-desert. god-boil. sun hot bright red neck. gold beat down bash your brando. tata ta-yogo. bird shape. the gateway: a geometrical structure. the appearance of one albinos. with garnet eyes. with love ray eyes. fluid transfer. light. clover. ta-ta carwreck ta-ta jeweled grass soular radio ta-ta. todo lingual. todo toda todda todd a. ta la ta ya ta na. no noe. noone. one know. know one noe

iii

the landscape is moving

easter

the body
the endless dunes
the glittering mineral salts
my being stark like a soldier
I cannot fast I must eat eat eat
the chalky golden paws of a lion
I don't care about art anymore
passion will pass thru the veins
stronger than the plastic creations of man
I embrace thee madman spiker
and slammer of the graceless pietà
as the shroud it exists
only as marble to kiss
as a relic just a relic
the stoned merging the kiss of Constantin
this is a rather foolish art lesson
alone in the study
in the looming vaults of ancients
I would pour over plates
of siennese madonnas
the languid primitives
the lilt and tilt of a modigliani
a mountain a monument
giving rise to laughing eyes
just a girl in green stockings
too anxious and ready to move
too quick to test the truth
everything is something else
a mouth is a wound
I violate with my pencil
the tip of my finger

the body of a canvas
the frescoes of florence
the porous skin of plaster saints
sweating bands and beads of love
all art seems pointless
one blurring photograph
an elusive face
or the face of christ
straining wax
rather to be a flaw
in the belly of an elastic ruby
making love on a carpet
red and vibrant
breath of babies suckle spit
in the face of a worthless tintoretto

we long for what we cannot love
to be freed from the boundaries
of our terrible skin
the tuscan sun
I long for life for italy
to cut my entrails
OUT
and wash them crystal
and wear them round my neck
to sup on purple blooms
shooting from swift teeth

The venetian gate clicks
beyond the drape lurks art
everything gradually connects
the mediterranean stretch
like a hand over a mouth
art has thou forsaken me

why hast thou forsaken me
I crouch and excrete
a mass of speckled clay
an oasis an orchid
a sleeping craft
in the trenches its war
porcelain faces chime
blue and shell like
wake up child arise
victory is a drug
that we take together
in the trenches
its lilies
gathered in stenciled arms
in the trenches its war
woman in black car
woman in dark glasses
what I don't see
is translated by God

1975–1976

neo boy

the son of a neck
rilke

everything is shit. the word art must be redefined.
this is the age where everyone creates. rise up nig-
ger take up your true place. rise up nigger the word
too must be redefined. this is your arms and this is
your hook. don't the black boys get shook. high
asses get down. nigger no invented for the color it
was made for the plague. for the royalty who have
readjusted their sores. the artist. the mutant. the
rock n' roll mulatto. arise new babe born sans eye-
brow and tonsil. outside logic, beyond mathematics,
self-torture and poli-tricks. arise in/health new nig-
gers and celebrate the birth of the one. this is your
calling and this is your psalm. rise up niggers and
reign w/your instruments of fortune.

everything comes down so pasturized
everything comes down 16 degrees
they say your amplifier is too loud
turn your amplifier down
are we high all alone on our knees
memory is just hips that swing
like a clock
the past projects fantastic scenes
tic/toc tic/toc tic/toc
fuck the clock!

Time is a woman reshaping, taking watch.
she perfumes her hair w/the attar of battle

her armor is the rose cut brass of allah.
bond or bondage
that is the question
arise! the people divided are not strong enough.
arise nigger we are summoned
by the panel of horns.
of the rim of horn and the space around.
spread w/hoops and hooves
and the grain of clarity and charity
he who challenges the king
receives commune and call
trial by riddle/trial by fall
communication of the future
is not in heaven
it's here man

je/hova I have
the son of time pieces it all together
the 17 jewels of the alchemist
a burning breast

Time is a myth
of gold and shit
like karat eggs easing out of goose ass
the long animal cry/woman is blessed
the perfect merging of beauty and beast
the green gas moving in like excitement
and the slip/slipping
sliding into layers of wax
red black gone and going
a woman alone in a tube of sound
resounds is resounding
a long low whine
moving thru the spine

a pelvic wind up
thru the primal arms
newboy is spawned
bald and screeching
like an eagle on a table
w/tongue preserved
coiling then flashing
a slender thread of lightning
piercing tense and shattering space
a woman gives birth to an ass and a face.

everything is shit. no i don't believe it. calligraphy
    glows.
inspired worms twine and emit a hairy rubbery
    light.
great hands twist and bend the strings and shoot
    high
sliming fugies thru comic neon. neo boy is born
    again
in the red and yellow torrents of rock n' roll shinar . . .

scrapbook green suit
standing over john
legs spread spurting gold
i was a hipster/revival
swinging chain
bending and bombing
the face of a finishing school
a fool leaning jukebox
altar kneeler
action painter
misery herself writhing on a bed
of pale blue mohair
there and not there

i was several others
and i was your mother
i manufactured your nectar
and moved from your presence
to worship your radiance
baby hold the lamp
my generous equal
baby hold the lamp
on my celestial body
the bells just vomit
the hard grunts
the magical moans
w/our duty union
and our sweet detachment
baby hold the lamp
shooting arrows shooting arrows
city of glittering architecture
city of endless spheres
moons of light—billowing face masks
city of minarets—city of stars—
amours—city of love and birth—of you
neo boy star of my belly.
each cry we utter is lost
if you killed ten of the people it wouldn't matter
if you save the son of a king it's worth a lot

i am your savior
i am your lover
i am several others
and i am your mother
who moves from your presence
my radiant
my eminent
epidemic

city of stars

christ! the colors of your energies.

neo boy melts in jelly machine. the whole thing is how he can change the scene or be changeling. transformation is relative says neo boy. tropical plants shiver. what can you say about habitat that hasn't been said before? greedy children lap up radio active jewels spit in the dunes by algerian know-it-alls. soon the gleaming bones of innocents will scatter the sands and some enterprising old jew will gather them up in an old leather bag and sell them to a contact. a roman woman, a catholic. a beautiful though childless shrew who will rearrange the bones with all the discreet adoration of a japanese boy adjusting his weapon. neo boy plucks up a sharp metal star and cuts a new scene from a sheet of copper. what can you say about habitat that hasn't been said again? lillies crown eyes. i'll soon be dead. condemned to total peace despite the long chain of unspeakable horrors i carve from a span of flat coil.

milky spirals boring in a clearing and ooze a message significant only to happy boys celebrating twin births. the frolic w/buck in miles of icing. pausing to let arrows fly from their birthday bows. a million darts pierce the ice forest evaporating crystal deer leap like melting eye of butter. neo boy just nods and laughs then slides deep in his machine messing with the multi-colored controls and merging with blue fish space. neon squiggles. squirl squaggle. yes! it's neo boy's electric spaghetti calligraphy. he's just signed his name to a perfect work of art—the sky.

bones of children and a nice winding fart blown
from the ass of neo boy—blow over the town called
bethlehem. all this shit over a town. antidisestablish-
mentarianism. against the church of england. he
readjusts the dials. everything explodes then rear-
ranges. landscape can be recreated says neo boy
proudly displaying his platform—one of the most
expansive on the planet. every town known to man
in perfect miniature. there is harrar. there is the
white stucco arena reserved for victims of plague
and memory and abandoned space where no one is
out of place here. where only a shapely waitress
would be out of shape here. let me out let's eat shit.
neo boy has a pain in his playing arm. must get him
his guitar. window breathes sigh of relief. no base-
ball thru me today. outlines pulse. its neo boy teen-
age alchemist. peel your winky-dink screens. neo
boy is coming. fu-ching will attempt to shake him up
with victorian chink tricks but our boy is steps
ahead with all the invisible guile of a sixteenth-
century jap/immortal kamikaze divine wind as-

signed to crash laughing. neo boy w/skin shimmer.
yellow rubber tissue fingers forming crazy moun-
tains etched in pink fluorescent shadows. flubber
shadow. paper flowers nodding rhyming bearing
red teeth. neo boy grins and leaps into the sea pom-
maded with blood. the sticky kisses. the wet and
shining lips of neo boy slobbering on his master. the
innocent worship. the exotic mathematics. the
music of neo boy popping electric exclamation
points from wet tongue of neo boy on commack
spleen rack. sliding home free like oiled baseball
thanks to oil droplets on the feathers of neo boy
craning his neck to aim sink and eat (not devour) the
moon. goo-rain la lune caught like a gas bubble in
the belly of neo boy dreaming of remarkable voyages
accursed ships frozen in dish shapes and his crazy
disgrace as he exits in a field of jazz.

city of stars city of glitter and architecture city of
endless spheres moons of light city of lost logics city
of love and birth . . .

the aquatic origins of neo boy marveling internally, his facilities and the facility in which he is able to project pictures. that old pine tree glows like cinema! scores of radioactive angels mugging for the camera. mugging and twisting in a huge white teepee—an erect parachute of salt frozen only a few feet away from the young blond pilot foaming in the snow. his mouth filled with the seven numb fingers and the two blue cereleum eyes of neo boy charging down a bright green hill drenched in armor of pale tissue. look out stadium here he comes! honey bears and gentle beasts cheer as he rips their tormentor (shape of an eight feet metal teethed monster) into lurking thunder. Yay! finger mouth is advancing. Yay! metal teeth is mincing words. Yay! neo boy wipes them all out with his atomic dusting cloth. the miniature animals saw horses and wavy deer frolic around the party cake. horses leap from their porcelain skins and the sky fills with numbers.

tired little boys have to go to bed. tired little boys are half sleepy, momma. no truths do they know but the truths i have told them. love and levitation nothing infrared is foreign. go, my sleepy boys. when they do not dream they vomit.

sohl

a cluster of glories erupted from his skull.
filled with holy dread he opened his chest
and removed a small oval hand mirror.
ivory and crystal and perfectly wrought. he
had intended to inspect his head but instead
dwelt for several minutes on the elegant
craftsmanship of the mirror. the ivory
had a rich grain, veins and in the center a
crack. he knelt and squinted so as to get
a better look. in the crack there was a garden.
it was so green that he fell down in laughter
and rolled and rolled over the cool blades.
the blood streamed and covered the amazing
fields. the pale glories, accustomed to worship,
reared their heads and let themselves be washed
in the ruby luxury. after several days of rain
and all traces of the man gone. the children
were let free to roam and gloat
in the long fields of poppies.

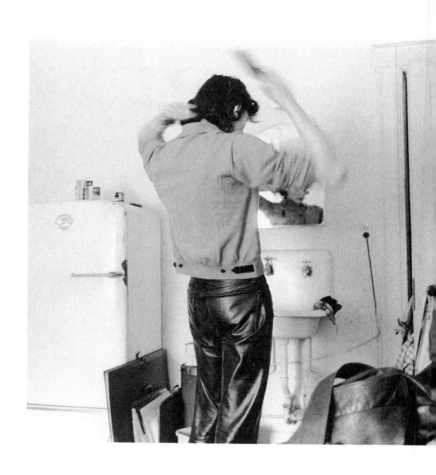

land (version)

*. . . the feel of horses long before horses
enter the scene . . .*

The boy was in the hallway drinking a glass of tea. from the other end of the hallway a rhythm was generating. a process of rude investigation. the hard glare stretched. he set down his glass. growth too is rude. the high grass indigo leaves. he lit a fag surveyed the terrain. the red air split. his nostrils twitched. his throat, filling with the phlegm of awareness, tightened over the sounds of his despair like a net over prey. wings fluttered against his chord and his enormous eyes rolled back. the leaves rearranged exposing his mission clear as a wavy bend. and the music . . . the music . . .

The boy is johnny has always been johnny . . . johnny bongo johnny cloud johnny guitar johnny o'clock. time is falling. he straps his boots and seizes his bag. he is johnny appleseed subliminal landscape painter. he is the brush the mouthpiece. he is gyrating on the edge of indifference. spinning off the cliff. seducing holy fists, pressing the lever of the lost. and who is found? he checks the glass. a sultry image who has shaved his fragile throat. with buttered hair and greased gestures. He buckles his cup lip hands pocket full of seed. he is his own steed ready to go man go man go and he knows how to pony as he dives into a triptych of sweat dedicated to nothing but the cultivation of a land of a thousand dances.

suite

the black screen. the glittering lights of the river.
the boy in black uniform high on a hilltop with his
hair blazing. the boy raises his arm to nature.
nature, restless and moody,
does the unspeakable—
she extends her hand.
a siren a sound so disarming
he lets go and is ravaged by sharkless teeth,
a set of teeth afloat in the ribbed waters. nature
in another time another period, caused them to be
extracted from her lover—the basking shark.

citizens! we must not sleep.
our sons are running like seasons to nature.
man the tower and trestle tenderfoot soldiers.
daughters! be awake at the wake
be you rigid and immobile and in guard.
citizens! resurrect your sons
from this sad spot of decay.

the woman the tree and the arms equal nature.
the cry is take me with you. rolling in beds of salt
within the agonizing dimension of stillness she is
coming. coming in his arms. coming in fiber.
i love you, whispers nature.
a ragged whisper like the threads of her gown.
a garment of water with the texture of dusting
powder. just as he would be kissed
by death he is falling back.
he must pull away he needs his hand.
his nose itches.

the granite lifts.
the angry swell of water charging into cloud
cloud is confused
clouds are rearranging
adjusting slate
silhouette of the boy and his mother
her hair is a mane of survival
her hair, plaited, is a weapon
she is the womb of return, the protractor
she extends her hand she ruffles his hair
she covers his head with a cap of black wool
the shock of iron the wailing of women
one night it will happen it will happen again
he is bound to step thru
humping the space
between death and death
the medieval trumpet
the clarion
the clarinet
a solo of holes
a boat of stardust
a laundress
notes bad and tender
and the claustral joining
encounter in space
the boy w/the black river
as he turns in the arms of nature
who worships the flaming sons of women

grant

i think it was on the sabbath, the day of rest, that
trouble was invented. the creator fell asleep and
dreamed. it was the first sleep and the first dream.
the dream of god. the primal pandora. from the sub-
liminal of the spirit arose monsters and artists. mas-
ters and the archangel.

today is sunday and i have spent some of it with my
father. the weather scares me but i like it. it's raging

out. my body hurts as it always does when the weather is bad. it came quite unexpectedly. the sky went black and it was hailing in the spring. i never know what it's going to be like anymore because he doesn't tell me. it used to be he'd call and say, "it's a storm here. you'll have it in two days." or "the sun is coming." i needed no other source but the word of my guardian.

we live for a very long time in our imagination for the misfit it is the light and heady alternative. the misfit is one who is true and troubled and filled with shining blood. but for my father the irrevocable alien, there is nowhere to go, unaccepted by the real world and betrayed by the divine, he has plunged into a state of atrophy. a trophy a stationary prize. it is the junky becoming the junk the dreamer the dream. it is the masterpiece himself. a/trophy.

god sleeps. his people—devout, ambitious and correct—regard the sabbath with complete charge and submission. being of one tongue and of one mind, mindful of him, they probed him delicately. their merging energies craved house, craved test and plunger. they materialized the first hypodermic. thus they were able to inject their concentration into the pit of his dreaming.

thus they were made intimate with the most intimate of the spirit. it was there that man communicated with higher orders and there he learned the great secrets. babel imposed unspeakable wrath. for they had learned the secret of levitation thru communication. the secrets of god, of architecture.

they became one with his specters, his archangels, and the sounds auraying the revelation.

for him it was a day of complete escape from his social involvement with his creations, the dilemmas of good and evil and of those not able. for him it was the time of precious truth. of dream.

i imagine god jealous and crazy—ribbed in neon day-glow. he just can't believe that his people, the ants, have tapped into him through the sabbath. he had exposed himself as a result of the harmonic alchemy that existed between his dreaming and their worshiping. he could not accept that they were so connected and so he caused them disconnected. man was condemned to wander the earth like hordes of leper telephones.

a gale, 20 mile winds. the rain.

i imagine and i dream. god sleeping. my father searching. god awakes and scoops him up and embraces him. there is the father—king kong and my father—the golden one.

today is sunday. i've spent it with my father. i have watched and listened and opened w/him. have shared his longing—his desire for perfect union. his disappointment in a destiny of wandering far from heaven. his resignation. his suffering the agony of losing his grip on the thread of dreaming. the final corrupting of his innermost dream by the invasion of the surveyors of reality.

I recognize him as the true outcast. he is lucifer the unguided light, judas the translator and barabbas the misused. so certain of gods existence he would attempt to deny, defy or seek him beyond the constricts of the law—the rock. I recognize a man with dark glasses, of medium height in a brown shirt. an acrobat, a runner, a factory worker, and the husband of my mother.

I recognize the tower of babel as a symbol of penetration. the symbol of a moment when man's desire to be close to god was so intense that he invaded his dreams. i recognize a man whose dreams have also been invaded and truly believe there is no one closer to god than my father.

december

perfect moon
I am calling
perfect moon
clad impure
I approach
your naked neck
barefoot
baying
perfect moon

perfect moon
I am with you
perfect moon
I adore
surrendering
to thy great
hands
I am yours
perfect moon

doctor love

love is a vampire. the dead facts. energy undead.
here in dreams he captures girls. the girls are left to
their own devices. a free society observed on lividio—
live video. the silvery brazen image of the collapse of
pure democracy. within the confines of his modern
fortress he charts the construction of the tiny female
state like a sociologist over ants/bees. Just as these
mad ones are able to find space w/the pearl and tray
of a florentine doily, so is doctor love able to depat-
tern their subtle intricacies into a sheet of cold logic.
once he has figured them out he does away w/them.

the lighthouse in the distance is hope. no one
reaches out. a girl in black silk capris bending over,

sobbing. he dissects and drains until he has each one
down. strange chances? nothing. these women
crave organization. the reward for their therapy is
extermination. love craves flaws, distinction. the
challenge of the wrath and whims of a real woman.
the arch of the ceiling collapses. i am in the laundry
room. there i am the target of investigation. there i
am the dirty linen, the kink in the machine. love is
impatient to remove us. a new crop of women is ar-
riving—raw and invigorating.

there is nothing intriguing about our group. they
were rounded from one class . . . a sorority w/the
exception of myself, a bystander. a band apart
schoolgirl. they search for something inside of me.
the way to turn me on. they look to switch on the
least likely candidate. i've never been anything but
trouble for everyone. the other girls regard me as a
gram of misfortune unsettling the delicate balance
of their destructive order. order here means death.
the perfect circulation of their cool unit presents the
proper UD flow, the food and prey of hakim love. all
incentive directives point to order. order, the cruel
drain. disintegration save the cells that join the cells
of the undead.

ii

for a while i drew but some found out about it and i
feared i'd be classified as an artist. i was afraid they
would find a place for me in their society and thus
perfect declare their state to the V———. their re-
ward—the sucking of their blood. all fluids rotating
in harmony within his ancient greedy veins.

i therefore stopped drawing. sometimes i slip away (like this moment) and take open my red portfolio w/the soft burlap ribbons. i like to run my hand across the skin of each drawing. they cannot classify me without evidence. a flash of sulphur and one by one they are consumed by flame. they cannot classify me as an artist. art ceases. i've stopped. i dream of escape.

4 december. love is in a bad humor. he rounds us up. he calls the role for extermination. i call to protest. i have defied order. there is nothing left of the artist. no mood of creation. the rules call for a fixed state. all eyes fix on me. he is agitated, distracted. yours is a new classification, an offshoot of sig. 101—artist. sig. 1016—mutant. it is sunday. the sabbath is observed. death begins monday. as he is reading thursday's list a man enters. love softens. he seems to have lost interest in us. his eyes connect w/the eyes of the stranger by a thin shaft of stars. white man on a rope. he fast assigns the cook, myself, and a few remaining for friday.

finished on friday. everyone back to work. i feel so lonely like i don't belong except involuntarily. just mute, alien. the old gentleman leaves. he gives me sympathy w/his eyes. but then all visitors do, sometimes i think even love . . . days pass. monday's girls go. tuesday morning the old man returns. he had spent most of his life as a serf here and now, as a free man, he chooses to die here. there is a curious sense of loyalty here to love. in truth i seem the only one who wishes to leave. the spark that jetted from the visitor is dead. he is dying. escape is relative. he is about to enter love's quarters. before he does he slips a small parcel in the pocket of my trousers. the pockets are lined w/silk and i feel a high itch through my system. his hard calloused fingers smooth my thigh through the lining. the parcel jingles and fills me w/light. i understand the gift is escape. he stares at me softly, then withdraws.

no one has seen. i guess. it's difficult to assess as no one reacts to anything. their capture, their sentence, a new recipe, shine, rain, all the same. no one resents me, no one sees me. i am not even a rebel. nothing. a mutant accepted. they are even bored w/the plague but i guard my sores, i cannot accept defeat. my desire to escape mounts, tuesday's girls gone. i'm getting overexcited. beads of sweat decorate my forehead. i am a crazy carvel. wednesday the death bells ring. the old man is dead. my blood implodes. my skin shells a mild inferno. i must keep my composure. my obsession, escape, is only slightly rattled by his death. i feel a cold dry kiss on my mouth. i inhale the vapors of dry ice. something has entered me. something stirs, jets. my face is charged. bones—vibrating, electric.

doctor love has little interest in wednesday's girls. it occurred to me that had they fought or cried they may have been spared. it never seemed to cross their minds. death was listless, routine. me—i was desperate, addicted. i could not eat, just shoot pilot after pilot of my deam of escape. that night i was filled w/fever. and honor too, for the parcel (which i constantly handled like a rosary) was my connection w/a blessed future.

thursday morning was a service for the old man. i felt my duty to attend. love was not openly distressed but i felt his loss. i bent down to kiss his cold wrists. i felt his sympathetic glance. i don't know. i was so distracted, the inane pitied victim of a habitual conspiracy.

alone and pounding i was sure someone suspected. it was too quiet. there was a continuous buzzing, a drone. for a while i was sure i had been bugged. an electronic device had been embedded in my nodes and temple. thursday's girls were taken away. a trainload of fresh ones arrived. tomorrow i would die. it had to be tonight. the vampire went to his quarters for evening repaste. the cook was praying. there i was against the wall, misfit full of faith. suddenly it starts rising from my shoes. knowledge . . . power . . . i've imagined . . . shot and reshot this escape for days. now it's about to be realized. image: dancing nude in a munich discotheque. opening like willing scissors for the hands of men. imagination is about to be realized. pulling against action is that dangerous fear of change. survival is stronger and i decide it must be now.

love will be retiring for the evening. the full moon will serve me light. it will also make me more visible. i unwrap the parcel. it's a baby bracelet of platinum beads strung on a silver wire. dangling is a tiny gold heart and a gold key. i remove the key and slip through the yards.

the spotlights are armed toward the windows. the fear here is not escape but assassination. my heart stops. love's silhouette just above me but i keep running. the night is bright, silent. holy skies sprayed w/large stars and the moon in full rein. i reach a hedge w/an iron door. trembling i open it w/the key. within there is another hedge, high and endless like the great wall. two enormous fat black pussycats appear. massive cheshires brushing my legs. i'm afraid of them. i don't know if they're allies or enemies. i chance it. i follow them. i'm following them.

they lead me to a wall. a section of the wall has a low carved door which gives easily as i push into it. i shimmy through. it's difficult. the cats slip after me. they are an ominous pair, evils from pandora's box. little time for guilt. i wonder, i run, i run like mad. fields are immense and bright. the moon lights the sky like an eternal match. my tears contain no salt. rhymes race through my feet, pounding black beat of my heart, black cat black bat. it's true there is a shadow stretched across the luxurious face of pie. i run i run. i pray the peasants won't return me. i pray i've escaped forever from the fortress of doctor love. i imagine the women in their starched linens, heads shaven, assigned and numbered, punctured and drained. i imagine the boy, opal, crying and siphoning the metallic substance from the ritual caldron into large silver vats. here and there picking out hairs and clots and small insects. i run i run, and then i see them. through the trees. horses. white red and spotted. one is waiting. a hard miniature appaloosa w/long yellow hair. i leap on her, a graceless but true movement and i ride like hell.

iii

now i've lost control. i become someone else's point of view. the eye of the camera pulls back. i am merely a movement in a long shot of horses, fields and trees. i am riding a predestined escape route. i understand i am the (escape) goat. i have unleashed two huge black candlesticks onto the altar of illusion. the fiery bat opens her wings of raging chiffon. soft frame of sky smoky yellow sky dawn and ground. lateral tracking. a castle. a woman w/long chestnut hair waits like a statue to be unveiled. her form caressed w/layers of silky flame. suddenly her face lights up and she brushes her hair.

voiceover: *she was happy. she was queen. she who devours the suckling pig and the mutant folds. she waited, sometimes forever, for one perfect flaw to arrive. to carve and suck and bless. coming to her was the jewel she had craved. was the knob in the canvas. doctor love sent a wave of lush fruit through her delicate glistening spine of crystal. his hand gently squeezed the rare compote of her spleen. i was entering the scene. she was happy. his queen. all too pleased that her wait was not in/vein.*

AFTER/WORDS

i was led into a miniature amphitheater of white por-
celain. the floor tiles buzzing like kinetic sculpture,
waving like the color patterns of Vasereley. columns
formed a large rectangle. dead center was a marble
slab fitted w/a raft of leather. they laid her on the
table. a green cone descended through the skylight,
a draft of roses through the open window her cos-
tume was covered w/petals. every woman in history
she was, and every womb in venture. i looked in the
mirror. i gave birth to alexander, i was his lover. war
paint formed on my face, ochre and lavender
slashes. the woman w/the chestnut mane stood over
her. her delicate hands worked small miracles. slen-
der celuloid tubes were swiftly inserted into the
pores of the victim, a virgin. the tubes were tentacles
melding w/her veins her dreams and deeper into the
virginal light, the pool beneath memory. a ruby flux
where no words were formed. the queen was a god-
dess strapping to herself a love mechanism—a de-
vice designed for penetration. a pointed cylinder of
jeweler's plat. i held back as long as i could. i was the
throne she was mounting. i was the seed of destiny,
the conceit of reign. first would be the poke, the
light, and then the kiss. a flood of steam and wire
released. i could not resist her face was connecting
w/my own. the rush and hiss of a mammal going
under.

—what do you want out of me? she said
—undulating I cried—lust!
—what do you want out of me? I asked.

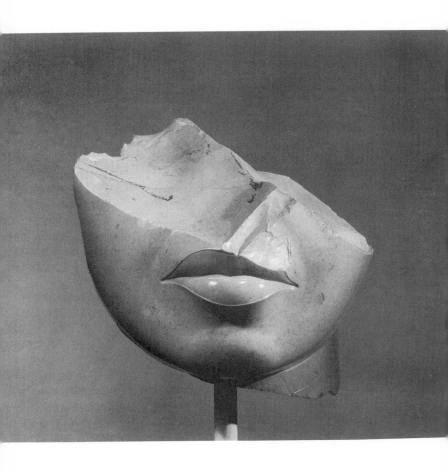

—language, she said, language.

ps/alm 23 revisited
for William Burroughs

The word is his shepherd
he shall not want
he spreads like the eagle
upon the green hill
boys of the Alhambra
in vivid sash
serve him still
your orange juice, sir
your fishing pole
accepting all
with tender grace
and besting us
with this advice
children never be ashamed
wrestle smile walk in sun
thank you, Bill
your will be done
God grant you
mind and medicine
we draw our hearts
and you within
moral vested
Gentleman

rimbaud dead

he is thirty-seven. they cut off his leg. the syphilis
oozes. a cream virus. a mysterious missile up the ass
of an m-5. the victim suffers soul-o-caust. his face
idiotic and his marvelous tongue useless, distended.

rimbaud. no more the daring young horseman of
high abyssinian plateau. such ardor is petrified for-
ever.

his lightweight wooden limb leans against the wall
like a soldier leisurely awaiting orders. the master,
now amputee, just lies and lies. gulping poppy tea
through a straw—an opium syphon. once, full of
wonder, he rose in hot pursuit of some apparition—
some visage. perhaps harrar a heavy sea or dear
djami abandoned in the scorched arena-aden. rim-
baud rose and fell with a thud. his long body naked
on the carpet. condemned to lie there at the mercy of
two women stinking of piety. rimbaud. he who so
worshiped control now whines and shits like a colic
baby.
now appointed now basket case wallowing in rice
waste. now muscular tongue now dumb never to be
drunk again. save tea time when he pulls the liquid
in. gasping it deludes the bloodstream. conscience
abandons him. he's illuminating kneeling climbing
mountains racing. now voyager now voyeur. he
notes it all. very ernest surreal oar. his artificial limb
lifts and presses space. limb in a vacuum.

does rimbaud beckon?

no he's gazing

in the wall is a hole. duchamp thumbprint pin light
fraction. an iris opening. gradually we see the whole
thing. everything opens unfolds like a breugal. it's a
holiday . . .

it's a wedding feast . . .

they're roasting pigs and apples apron. the odor is
rising. it's sunday it's manet it's picnic in the grass.
it's a seurat time it's light time it's the right time for
romancing for canoeing and for dancing.

and rimbaud's limb, being so caught up, goes be-bop-
ping out the door into the forest through the trees—
raga rag in the grass overturning picnic baskets
whizzing past churchyard gates right in step it
genuflects then aims and leaps over the scene over
the rainbow out of the canvas into space pure
space—as remote and colorless as dear arthur's face.
a face made incorporeal full of grace. sunken eyes—
those cobalt treasures closed forever.

clenched fist relaxed wrist
his pipe turned in . . .

out in the garden the children are gathering.
it's not a whim. they are accurate immaculate,
as cruel as him.
they sing:
legs can't flail
cock can't ball
teeth can't bare

baby can't crawl
rimbaud rimbaud facing the wall
cold as hail dead as a doornail

sudden tears!

thermos

(radiant coins)

love was in a constant state of liquid grace. love was
the warm and waxy elixir transported in the cool
mercurial regions of a thermos. thru the stark shad-
ows she would crawl, the thermos between her
knees. the edges of her pantaloons hot and billow-
ing. there were smooth golden tears embedded in the
flesh of her thighs. glowing stains of other such
vigils. she'd shimmy from the sleep of harem into
the austere recesses of the Rea désheed military bar-
racks. sometimes the boiling coffee would overflow
and shock the silk of her cloth and waist. still she'd
go on until the thick and unmeasurable warmth
would reach the lips and throat of her one most be-
loved.

one night she was taken for a deserter and shot. the
load dropped from her shy trappings and hit rock.
she was able to retrieve it and make her way to the
penile chamber—his prison. she felt free only when
she was with him, so she chose to drop there in total
submission before him. in the center of his grief
there was her offering. as always he unscrewed the
lid and took a long draught. uncertain of anything.
save the end, he was unable to decipher the code in
agony of the gesture of her right hand. nor was he
able to comprehend the twitching of his lids and
hips. nor any spasm at all as the liquor and liquid
glass cracked, chipped, and made its slow slivery
silvery way through his bloodstream.

the ballad of isabelle eberhardt

I need a harem of men
so many rhythms within
my insatiable spin
the wind the sand
the worlds I embrace
the hottest place
the sad hospital
of my soul
billows as I roll
the terrain of new skin
I condemn any pattern
I bind I blend
other sedatives cigarettes
vines twisting under belts
of the female nerve

I need a harem of wisdom
time trickling wit
sinking blood of scareb
the crescent wound
A life ago
I petitioned a harem
of gods and was struck
in the neck
the great weight
the flake of idols
bobbing heads of gods
rendered in the saber
of relinquished hearts
disbanded hands

My throat a vehicle
I have moved from the caravan
to spread myself at your feet
I have vowed
to meet thee
in the belly of a rock
the last thing I'll see
is your stare within me
a liquid stretch
obscuring stench
that I may pass
from this existence
knowing I existed
holding fast the gold plate
the koranic script of stars

I need a raft
to carry me over
the yellow river
a harem of prayers bells
chiming Isabelle
the ballad of a girl
the drunken violin
who drowned in the desert
wrapped in her name
dressed in sheets
of her own fair hand
waves of muslin
one last word
Islam I am
devour me
Lord

corps de plane

i

we came into this area quite accidentally. there was no overwhelming suspense, no compelling drama. we simply drifted over and landed. on sand. our vessel sunk very quickly with no sound. the others removed their shoes. i had none and walked ahead, alone. my companions took an alternate route into adventure and i never saw them again. i was alien, alone. with no misgivings or regrets. we landed like a dream so i allowed the future to unfold like the petals of a seductive and sinister flower.

gravity was with me. i barely touched ground. therefore the burning granules did not harm me, only made small rude pits on the bottoms of my feet. these i caused to melt away, like expiring goggles in the dunes. i couldn't bear the marring and pitting of my elastic feet. in the clouds the men were performing their dizzying escapes. bomber pilots going up in red smoke. the explosions descended into a breeze that blew up my skirts. several layers of khaki chiffon lifting and revealing the wanton muff of a flower.

i am armed with sweating memory. beads of information like cartridges on a leather strap. revolution is one of our most charming commodities and the sands respond. revolt and swirl beneath my feet. strain and wave in the shape of a long and lapping tongue. i could not speak. i was trained to give, not receive, pleasure. there i was overcome. glistening

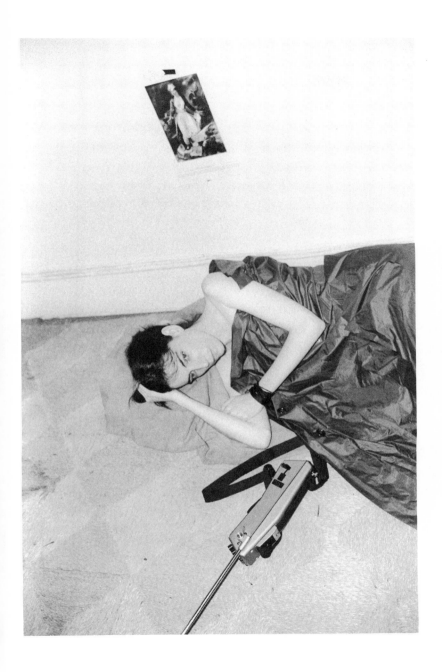

hairs of the desert were aggressively clogging my pores. i was stretched out. i was jamming with the experts. sucking with the fibrous rhythum of the sand. the sand, first intrigued, was soon involved.

ii

there was a distinct pain in my right shoulder. i could hardly bear it. overhead, men with glowing helmets, carved up the city on a flat easel. the tri-color sketch of the final divisions were only an arm's length from the long funeral curtains behind which i was hiding. 3-D biplanes in the distance. the men gathered by the window sucking their pipes and dis-cussing the approaching craft. i reached for the plans. the pain was excruciating. i bit down on a capsule. overhead was the syndicated formation of enemy planes. one of the adrenal people flashed and flooded the sky with light.

we were waging a war of aerial design. the simple symmetrics of the chromatrope were sent back to base for analysis. i was given the clipped black tube for the insertion of priority information. i was very tired. i was amazed and making it. free and naked. invisible runner breaking thru the front with the blueprint of the future wrapped in foil. i was given a coat of ribbons and kissed on the neck by the gen-eral. here i am alone in my tent with no servant nor invention of amusement. i have little use for the war games of man. what i was searching for was as sin-gular as radar. a brother—a dead woman—a shirt of electric hair.

what does it matter what I say? it's what i think that counts. planes of the human body. formation of a

glacier and the long thaw. desire for the word oblit-
erates the image. once my face is removed i am free
to plunge sans identity into a pure investigation into
sound. sound. a condition so abstract that i can al-
most taste what it feels like to utter the letters of
your name.

iii

a child is watching a war movie. the bomber pilots
have a 50–50 chance and they know it. there is noth-
ing to loose. victory is on the other side of boredom.
i am watching the same movie. it fills me with anxi-
ety, agony. the moves of these brave faces reduce my
own adventures to the mere turnings of a petticoat.
what experience could i enter that could compare to
this?

iv

i awoke. i tossed off the blush pads. my free eyes
understood. the light made my eyes twitch. i was
annoyed, violated. i was also the possessor of an
enormous appetite. i mechanically pulled the long
velvet tassle that was hanging to the left of me and
waited.

moody, sullen, uncaring where i was, i entered into
the game of the written. and it was written that i
should awake here and with servants. indifferent,
inimicable and a servant myself. a maid of the fu-
ture.

babelfield (version)

"we know how to give our whole life everyday"
a. rimbaud

wherein war is expressed
thru the violent hieroglyphs
of sound and motion
a scream is a shoulder
the profile of life
raised are our instruments—sonic necks
lubricants of aggression and flesh
notes pierce the body round
wounds are cherished blessed and bound
by boys posed before the spinal region
of the parthenon . . .
holy terrors—naked,gloved
spraying random verbs of love
and guerre on shining columns
we embody the ancient frieze
we are art/rat
filthy pups
we breed action
words we use up
grind into powder—volumes of sand
sifted as power death and breath
the elective irritant ticking
iris orifice the smooth throat
our component of charm
all that we gain
the awakening grain
the necessary agent for transmitting
the wave crashing the shackled gate
only the thumb of the father can undo

the great lock or raise the high tree
with weapons akimbo we seek said finger
we track the bolt housing all fate
we ritualize motion—gesticulate
we offer our arms wound in rags
we offer our eyes—pearls before sun
only the father can remove the particle
drape us in linen soften our necks
some of us serve as crusaders and some
as flies squashed against a fence
we live a spartan existence
when we were seven the military swept
us away like merchants of venus
knighted us implanted our instruments
of battle and babble
what is art/rat?
self-crucifiction
high on the hills are the camps. high camps.
high tribes. 14 stations and beyond the rock
a dream of sound. beyond the throat of man.
a violent claw stretching and scoping
the extended organ of god.
the tower is the symbol of penetration.
there was no actual structure save the image
of two parallel lines proceeding to point
vanishing hands in prayer
forming reforming and feeling the finger
do you believe in god?
he is my trainer
i was trained to run toward a ribbon of tension
attention! i was trained to run line and to face
and feed the front. to offer the hoof and tongue.
on the cots prostrate soldiers scream
no sound grasping sky writhing

pulling the rims of their ears like horns
there was too much traffic too much pain
i couldn't plug in i couldn't plug in
anywhere so i hid my amp in the bushes
and threw my guitar over my shoulder.
it weighs less than a machine gun
and never runs out of ammunition.
i rejoined my command we crawled the dunes
we slid over the hot mounds like coins
the grains, pocking our silk camouflage,
acted as irritants arousing our flesh
words we use up
only four remain
attached with the symmetrical luck of a clover
sound is the final analysis of an equation
involving X and intuition
sound is the healing worm
injected in the underbelly
the tongue of love
communication
with heaven
is here man
the penetration
the eye of butter son butter
which we dread and spread on our hair
we grease and wage war with fat roman cats
we fall on our knees
we jack our strats
rings radiate eardrum
distended skin trumpets
your opiate is the air you breathe
and the way you manipulate
your particles of charm
here i am empty warrior

here i am stripped of ribbons
of honor of rhythum
here i am utterly bruised by finger
here i am broken of figure of speech
here i am reeling and like a small fish returned
here in formation in taps on the field
sands are littered with monuments
with guitar necks like bayonets
testaments of truce and debt and sweat
i raise my guitar to the sky. i hold it in/pawn
with my two hands. i kneel and return to the note
of service. the scream it makes is so high pitched
that nobody hears save the herd of sound.
save the clowns of heaven
guiding the fold
and granting us wisdom
the kingdom of bliss
the lord is my shepherd i shall not want
me i just laugh i reel from my amp
the bush is in flames
but i could care less
i'm in a hurry
i don't plug in
i'm at the finish
i'm finishing
i step up to the microphone
i have no fear

babelogue

i haven't fucked w/the past but i've fucked plenty w/the future. over the silk of skin are scars from the splinters of stages and walls i've caressed. each bolt of wood, like the log of helen, was my pleasure. i would measure the success of a night by the amount of piss and seed i could exude over the columns that nestled the P/A. some nights i'd surprise everybody by snapping on a skirt of green net sewed over w/flat metallic circles which dangled and flashed. the lights were violet and white. for a while i had an ornamental veil. but i couldn't bear to use it. when my hair was cropped i craved covering. but now my hair itself is a veil and the scalp of a crazy and sleepy comanche lies beneath the netting of skin.

i wake up. i am lying peacefully and my knees are open to the sun. i desire him and he is absolutely ready to serve me. in house i am moslem. in heart i am an american artist and i have no guilt. i seek pleasure. i seek the nerves under your skin. the narrow archway. the layers. the scroll of ancient lettuce. we worship the flaw. the mole on the belly of an exquisite whore. one who has not sold her soul to god or man nor any other.

1977–1979

high on rebellion

what i feel when i'm playing guitar is completely
cold and crazy. like i don't owe nobody nothing and
it's a test just to see how far i can relax into the cold
wave of a note. when everything hits just right (just
and right) the note of nobility can go on forever. i
never tire of the solitary E and i trust my guitar and
don't care about anything. sometimes i feel like i've
broken through and i'm free and could dig into eter-
nity riding the wave and realm of the E. sometimes
it's useless. here i am struggling and filled with
dread—afraid that i'll never squeeze enough graph-
ite from my damaged cranium to inspire or asphyx-
iate any eyes grazing like hungry cows across the
stage or page. inside i'm just crazy. inside i must
continue. i see her, my stiff muse, jutting about in
the forest like a broken speeding statue. the colonial
year is dead and the greeks too are finished. the face
of alexander remains not solely due to sculptor but
through the power and magnetism and foresight of
alexander.

the artist preserves himself. maintains his swagger.
is intoxicated by ritual as well as result. look at me
i'm laughing. i am lapping S from the hard brown
palm of the boxer. i trust my guitar. therefore we
black out together. therefore i would wade thru
scum for him and scum is ahead but we just laugh.
ascending with the hollow mountain i am peaking.
we are kneeling we are laughing we are radiating at
last. this rebellion is a gas which we pass.

the salvation of rock

for Fred Sonic Smith

rock, like sculpture, is the solid body of a dream. is an equation of will and vision. the marble poacher pushes and tests the grain then strikes in the space and manner best accommodating his ultimate purpose. he is working from the akimbo plane. from the archery of angles. the chiseled tip of the arrow merges w/the target. pioneer ships bloat and explode. the universe is in/flamed w/the passions of man. streaking the sky is a chrome troller of remarkable speed and luster. the high cranial of mill pogany. 1920. polished brass. seventeen inches. no face no mouth no wall of speech. simply a head. a breathing helmet.

the headress is obsolete. and perhaps language, like this bitching reference, is also finished.

i am being paid to speak so i speak. elsewise i would create only for lust. the ghosts that surround vision are moving in. they are filling our craniums w/the dust of huts. adobes and aggies. genius is asleep in a cave of marble. over there on the stone base lies genius-lidless and heavy w/the smoke that makes from the pipe/line of past glories.

it was brancusi who had the courage to crack and reconstruct the intelligent innocence of an egg. thru mold and concrete he shot the perfect shape into rock. the hard gold thrust of a feather.

Constantin Brancusi, *Bird in Space*. (1928).

the shape of a feather is the essence of flight. the indian, true levitator, took this feather and another and others. fashioning a bonnet of plane.

crazy horse had one such feather. with it he scratched the shape of a bolt into the knees of a dreamer. blue eyes reached out. blue eyes scoped further. blue eyes focused a rock—a smooth stone which he caught up in leather and tied thru his ear as a gesture of promise.

he that plunders pays. once he bent down to pick up a diamond. he was shot in the knee and his knee opened and streamed the tears and words of his people. he wept and pissed and attempted to abuse his spoil and recapture the language of the lost.

here he gripped his ear and the ear of his horse.

he rode very fast and the wind whistled thru his wound. he manipulated the pain and reinvented the cliff and the waterfall—the totem of the redeemed. he proved the hand that pulls positive raises. hear then the levitation of the rock is truly possible.

stoned in space. zeus. christ. it has always been the rock and so it is and so it shall be. within the context of neo rock we must open our eyes and seize and rend the veil of smoke which man calls order. pollution is a result of the inability of man to transform waste. the transformation of waste is perhaps the oldest preoccupation of man. gold, being the chosen alloy, must be resurrected—via shit, at all cost. inherent within us is the dream and task of the alche-

mist. to create from clay a man. and to recreate from
the excretions of man pure and soft then solid gold.

all must not be art. some waste we must disinte-
grate. positive anarchy must exist so that we may
come to know and resist and grow beyond the an-
cient shape of a feather.

what is a hero?
—a silent indian
—a uranian guerilla
—a hard and heartless abstract expressionist
—or a little girl with glasses

somewhere in america, in a certain state of grace,
there exists
one who never sleeps except at light.
one who falls and one who fights.
one who salivates on the rock of right.

hymn

we hadn't eaten in two days. we were entirely intox-
icated. for me it was his presence, the alcohol and the
glow of communication. i couldn't bear to fill up
with anything but liquids while he was near me. nei-
ther of us was able to eat. i had a soft dose of hashish
which i washed down with calvados. i watched his
hand grip the slender neck of the bottle.

the hash was coming on and i couldn't function. he
led me to the door and saw me to the station. i was
trying to vomit but there was nothing in my stom-
ach except for a few crackers. we made no plan of
contact. the bus pulled away and some nuns skirted
across the window. i got involved with the hem of
their dresses—a perfect round of socket stitches. i
didn't get a last glimpse at him. i was a human bomb,
a greased and mushrooming drill. the bus was mov-
ing into a black hole. i didn't resist. i saw his face and
relaxed and left. i was gone. when the bus landed the
driver came and got me. the car moved slow and
wicked through the dense fog. it was thick and wavy
like the breath of a beast. i could smell jasmine. the
monastery was up ahead. the silence and beauty of
the tomb of charm. i couldn't talk, i was paralyzed.
in the bathroom i threw up in a trash basket. i rinsed
it out and caught my reflection in the mirror. it was
him and only him etched and soaked in the muscles
of recognition. i braced myself against the ledge of
the window and watched the mulled turnings of the
novices below. fragile monks with necks smooth and
cool like the skin of a magnum. pink bubbles drifted

from the mouth of the youngest, lying with his face against a rock. the other boys kept turning devout and burning and trilling a long gush of sounds and verbs that were easily transferred into a song of mutual love.

munich

it was all a dream. i hadn't washed my hair for forty days for forty nights. hennae locks hung heavy and greasy about my shoulders. i laid back and the woven mass stenched across the pillow, porous and sad. the blue light made my hands look transparent. the pink and yellow lights were sucked up by my greedy braids. a faded shot of falconetti beseeched me. typed over her grainy yeux were old words partly clouded by dying palms.

maria fake	tier du sange
renee falconetti	that circle circles
i'm mad for you	your morphine eyes
your death in life	raccoon raccoon
in film as jeanne	your morphine eyes
darc of light	like two wet balls
dry yellow palm	you got balls
crown of thorns	you got balls
line of blood	

her head shaven, etched with language, was a stark delicacy—a way out. i pulled myself up. my night shirt was stained. everything was caked with skin and sweat. the head of my lady consumed, shined. i rose with effort, filled with joy. one seized with a plan. i moved toward the wall. the tie that bound us together was fever. i did a turn. i was looking for scissors but i was immediately distracted. i moved toward the wall. i reached out and smoothed my hand across the grain. it was georgian, eighteenth century. a writing desk dominated by tiny arches and secret compartments. in one was a passport. in one was a tower, a miniature of the ziggurat of babel and a sapphire of india. red and black. i pulled the cloth from the window. the light flooded the room with such urgency that i started laughing. the stone had a star in its navel. i played with its nostrils, lubricated them with stardust, then moved over to my other things and other times. an agfa lupe 8X for magnifying sections of photographs. pociao-bonn. richard sohl-new york. brian jones in black and white banquet. a barbarian in scotland. i was coming in focus. i found the scissors. my locks fell in clumps on the floor. i tore thru the drawers. all this action in a few seconds. a rubber stamp, tattoo ink and numbers. double sevens shone from my cropped skull like a radiant scar. i felt lucky, completely new and cut off from the possessive grip of my previous existence. long periods of insomnia bouts with fever and death small and breath/taking.

it took a long time for me to clean myself because the heat in the shower made me dizzy. i leaned against the tiles and stretched out my left arm. i pressed my palm hard against the enclosure and very slowly, so i wouldn't notice, i'd spicket the water pure froid— cold as you can get it. i had the urge to shit voltaire style, so i stood and pushed and squeezed my eyes until the long clay turd drooped and dropped and hit the porcelain shaft. i watched it slowly make its way down the drain. i washed my feet in the white bowl, dried and dressed myself in a fresh suit of linen. there were several hundred pounds in the dresser as well as sheafs of uncut francs. there were no marks. everything fresh. mint. i unrolled my scabbard. in a scarf of red leather i wrapped the money, my sebsi and the first book that filled me with ecstasy. once again fever saw it dominate my senses. once again i had successfully escaped its limitless boundaries. i leaped thru the frame into the canvas of nature. i was a specter of ryder; a raging maniac streaking like cheetah into the hysterical fire.

ii

the heavens were still and cold. my teeth were chattering and i was damp with sweat. it was breaking. i was ok. i spread the red skin over me and used the dough as a pillow. i had no need of memory. the stars were sockets; were militant doughnuts. the field was dotted with land mines and loaves of bread. i broke one open. its guts were white, pulpy and pitted with deep purple seeds. hard insects shining and cracking under the pressure of my thumbnail. the cloud meat i ate. i filled and bloated and i rose. eventually i burst in/reign. the rain rendered the mines ineffective. i covered my head and ran in safety under a tree shaped like a teepee. out of habit i shook out my hair. it shocked me to find it gone.

in my pocket was a helmet of pink felt. i brushed it and hung it on a branch. the sun was shining. it was may day and in the distance the guardians of innocence were wrapping poles with satin streamers. i was reminded of the terror and beauty of a garden. the rose garden of my grandmother. the screen door was like the ocean. i was pressing my face against the mesh gazing across to afrika. ebony women were carving legs for tables. gleaming legs smeared with honey. i think it was honey because it was sticky. i felt fat and sick. i had eaten too much bread. i leaned against the side of a white framed house and puked. i had lost my dog tags. my shoes were gone and so was my money. over there, stuck, in the branches, was my head gear. i smoothed it out and put it on. i felt better. i was clean and shiny like the cheek of a lacquered apple. i was healthy. a fresh foot soldier. my sleeves and pantlegs rolled. my socks down. i looked beyond and another gleam revealed where i had been lying. i gathered my stuff and moved on.

are you an artist by any chance?

no

freelance?

no

no-no no-no no-no-no
no-no-no no-no no no

i ran in indian rhythm. i ran for a long time with no fear nor destination. i just ran. like in/training. i was preparing for the marathon. i was a face in the newsprint breaking ribbon. suddenly i wasn't a rabbit anymore. i needed a goal. the runner returns to the stadium. i wasn't returning anywhere. one sharp moment of recognition. there was a splinter in my hand from the screen door. i had matches and a hem full of safety pins. i sterilized one and worked the splinter out. it was coated with gray enamel that refracted the sun.

this area was sparsely populated yet all the houses were identical. white framed houses with enamel roofing and siding. a girl is standing in the kitchen looking thru a screen. everytime her uncle takes her picture she squints. the sun reflects off the slick enamel and hits and shatters where she's been looking. i can barely make her out. for me getting my picture taken has always been uncomfortable. i feel too familiar with the camera; an eye that connects and freezes the present with one acoustic wink.

girl at bible school. girl in pleasure. girl standing in line at recess with an open face waiting to receive like sanction a big spoonful of raw honey. the sight of it made me sick. and i didn't like us all sucking off the same spoon. though we picked berries together i felt no sense of brotherhood. some of them i wouldn't even breathe with. sometimes i had to hold my breath in time with the exhaust on the bus. everything was returning, gushing and chattering out of synch like a home movie. soundtrack is the muffled voices of women. words projecting from the glazed faces of my ancestors. the green eyes of margarite and her madness. the slow, untimely death of a gentle woman. jessica, diaries and a harp.

music permeated the room like an odor like the essence of a flower. my sister was advancing; her mouth full of rose petals. is awareness evil? she was mischievious, wondrous. protected by an aura of innocence.

hours pass. where is my transistor? i'd like to hear the idiot. i like how the word idiot comes only once

with a sonic beep punctuating it. the cut night club-
bing. i imagine aliens moving in on a munich disco-
theque and injecting the air with jelly. a victim is
chosen. a victim is one of the chosen people. a victim
is stretched across the hump back of a volvo and as-
saulted by parallel vocals—one frontal, one sublimi-
nal. the one in the background is the one you get
your orders from.

i think i'll set up camp. repetition of a former formal
formula. the money pillow, the long smoke and the
book. the book takes the place of music. i have no
idea where i am and no desire to ask. i am in munich
and light is falling. i have a flash of inspiration. i dig
a hole and line the soft earth with english pounds. i
dump my stash and cover it over with the skin and
leaves. i've stuffed several sheets with francs inside
my shirt. i hail down a car and entertain the driver
in exchange for a ride into town. I pay for an amp, an
electric guitar, cords, picks and a strap. i promise to
return in a few hours. i get me a hot plate, a weight
of paper and a typewriter. in a remote section of
town i find a room. it needs white washing so i offer
pleasure to one of the local boys. he works as a
waiter not far from this place in a rock n' roll club.
he works for me but won't take anything in ex-
change. he brings me liquor and chewing gum and
says maybe next time.

the shops have closed. i can't pick up my purchases.
i lie down on the single bed and look up at the ceil-
ing. suddenly i feel dirty, agitated. if i were in rif, i
would slip into my burnoose and barter with the
night merchants. i grab a buttery jacket of chocolate
leather and make my way down the dismal commer-

cial streets. if this were somewhere else i should be returning with my arms loaded with oils and spices and bundles of mint. i walk for a long time. there is no one around. i am lost in the solar system of a modern german condominium. i hail a cab and have him drop me by the ramp of the club YES. i don't stay long because the women are giving me trouble. one gives me her necklace, one gives me everything. i take her in a car parked out in back. the music is loud and boring. the lights strobing. i am grateful for her stupidity, her pretty dress and her quaaludes. she looses control and drops a shoe. inside a wad of german marks which i palm. she opens for a kiss and i insert a small pink eraser. i leave her cursing and gagging and exit with my angel on his motorcycle.

the essence of motorcycling is to be free. i have developed a taste for fear and since this taste i crave the drama of competition, the dilemma of drugs and the dangerous glowing pit of communication called love.

i am not surprised we are going far away. far from my room far into the night. nothing surprises me. not his gestures, his silence, his coat nor our ride like an endless solo. a violent fuzz-tone. an organ coming on like orchestra. my lungs expand. i feel fine. my hairs grown in. i look like the dark side of a dutch boy. i feel happy i really feel great. i would like to be a guitar solo. one that resounds like bagpipes or bells. i would like to be the backside of a rickenbacker smashing against a limestone wall in replay on a raging newsreel.

IN ANOTHER DECADE ROCK AND ROLL WILL BE ART

we blew opium, brown bagged and reed piped. i knew exactly what he was going to do. he cradled my head then caressed and snapped my neck. i lay there unconscious but i knew what he was doing. every moment. he took the money and my wrist-watch and the keys to my room. he kissed me all over. the stars were huge in the clear black sky. the fields were bright with starlight. i was trapped in the nocturnal landscape of an impossible soldier. i could feel his hands around my neck. and his fingers smoothing and manipulating the muscles that stretched over the bone of my collar. i exhaled as he pulled. my lungs were full of water. it was raining. the stoic night rains of europe.

i was covered with mud. the grass had stained the cloth of my uniform. i walked for a long time in the rain until all traces of grass and sweat vanished. my wet translucent garments clung to my damp skin. dawn came with the sun. i was dry but i was unable to locate my original campsite. i hitched a ride back into town. i rode in the back of an open truck with four boys. each one gave me something. a mirror for signaling, a comb, a pair of brown shoes and a paper wallet. i braced myself against the panels as the oldest ripped the inner seams of my slacks. this way it was more like a skirt. they baste stitched the back and added a large red neckerchief to the front. all this action and i'm not moving. i was thinking of the night and what had happened. they were pinning my new skirt together, rolling down my socks and wrapping wild flowers around a crown of wire. all this movement directed toward my waist and head yet i remained motionless. i was gone. i was traveling.

i was rolling in the cornfield with my angel. the twist of wire slid down and encircled my neck. my tears caused it to rust then dissolve. the immediacy of this action scared the men. they yelled for the driver to stop and waved me off. i wandered aimlessly into the long drone of a velvet gown. the train seemed to go on forever. after a time i reentered town still in rags. in the center of town there was a fountain. water streamed and increased. i knelt down into the stream where scores of tadpoles rushed. the slimy algae twisted around my knee and down my calves jetting blue arteries over white clay. i washed my legs. there were scratches all over them. i picked some blossoms and fashioned myself a tiara of flowers. i looked at myself in the clear water. i had no opinion of my face. i was bred for a higher system of vanity. i was exhausted. i returned to my room.

the military blankets and the olive hopsacking on the windows are gone. everything is fresh and sweet, bathed in the afternoon light. there is a lead crystal decanter on the sill. i pour myself a thimble full of sherry, wash and retire naked on the bed. i relive it all over and over.

i was a narrow waving tulip. i slept for several hours. when i awoke he was standing there, watching over me. the amp was there and the guitar was there. he grabbed my feet and we started laughing

and kissing. we were both very happy and made love
quickly. like a salutation. he fell asleep inside of me.
i eased out of bed. there was no reverb on the amp so
i washed my hair instead. it was down to my shoul-
ders and the color of copper. i cut it crusader style. i
drew a thin blue line connecting my eyes and a verti-
cal line down my forehead thru the center of my
nose. i washed again then i washed his feet. he was
still and dreaming. i gathered his clothes in a bundle
with the exception of his blue coat. i could not imag-
ine him without it. i draped it over the wicker chair
and brushed the collar with the assured strokes of a
chambermaid. he was lying there in a wrinkled
shirt. the contours of his shirt crumpled like news-
paper. adrenalin coursed thru me. a jagged racer
charged thru my veins. my fingers were sausages—
shiny and pulsing—full of crazy energy. the guitar
felt good in my hands. i didn't plug it in. i was racing
with time and memory. i imagined him standing be-
side me concentrating on disintegration and bend-
ing notes. we were on the stage in a stadium and the
lights were low and mean. i was in a state of tempo-
rary surrender. song on the radio: bend for thee. i
am bending in half in service to him, for myself, for
the moment and soon everything is forgotten. mem-
ory is replaced with energy. i am moving through a
dense landscape lush and tropic. i am bending like a
manic willow, like a finger in pain. only the moment
and beyond the moment exist. sleeping he knows it
and dead so he would also know it.

iii
his clothes i sacrificed. i salvaged nothing. i bor-
rowed a small motor bike and rode out of town. pass

the long shopping plazas. pass the spaced out beauties in purple half boots. pass the sex shops and the downtown club with its aluminum stage like the belly of a broiler. i rode for a long time trying not to conjure his face—his consuming face and his silence.

suddenly i was free. let it go i laughed and i did. i let it all go with a rush and a moan of truth. my next piece of luck was a landmark. a frame house with gray enamel siding. soon i was able to locate my belongings. everything intact but the muddied lining. i was happy to have retrieved my soft burden. i slung it over my shoulder and pushed the bike over on its side in the open field. existing within my consciousness and deeper—embedded in the realm of dreams and of fever—are our encounters past and future. as for the present he is always inside of me. as for future—perfect soon i would be stopping to have a rest and have a smoke.

everything eventually repeats itself. in the cool breath of dusk i already sense a point of boiling. perhaps there is a mutual lack of edge. i have a last smoke. tears not words pour. something is brewing, however vague. it is there lurking like a saint in the thick of the eucalyptus. deep and dense encounter with many little deaths. munich. it was not the first time i had left a guitar behind nor would it be the last.

health lantern

i want you to be healthy. i want you to project the light of safe keeping. i also want to be feeling all the destructive rhythums in your body. i want your cough to disintegrate into sex. i want you to fuck and fuck me w/the same insistency in which you are fucked by your cough. i want to translate your cough into a laugh and laughter into a gasp and gas into jet. i want you to beat off in the ozone. cataclyme dangerous mountains. scale the airways of andes. i want you to lay w/your face to the ground. to eat dirt and make love and never cough again, so that we may dig all regions and ridges and gather the remains of all that inflames into the sack of the jaw.

penicillin

(living gods)

i have been lying here for a long time in stillness. it is dark, complete. a room full of steamy warmth. around the bed is comic debris—glowing, metallic. within i am dense cold press. sick, immobile. i can't get a grip or feel. am i lead or cloud? gravity is mysterious, ambivalent. milk ebbs thru my veins—sluggish and rich. salamanders dip and move forward.

there is no wind. i have a police whistle in place of throne (scream). i am unable to speak or sing. how sad everything is. the glands in my throat are throbbing eggs. sinking into a fresh pillow is a miraculous pleasure. i bless my bedding.

the physician entered, cool and needy. he gave me medicine of health, mold of trust, because he did not understand i was suffering from a malady of the spirit.

i loved him but i could not go w/him. we were condemned always to meet, to collide. my love filled him w/revenge. i had nothing of his in my possession, no photograph or cloth. nothing, not even memory. lying here my precious objects include a white handkerchief and a vial of maroon and gray capsules. the handkerchief is the barest egyptian cotton. a gift from a woman, a corsican. it has served as a wrapper for a broken angel. the angel i set w/my books. on the wall is a vellum sheet from the ivory coast. this morning it slipped from the wall and the angel—

shot w/antibodies—took on the aura of skim. someone joked that cortisone injections would build tissue and eventually regenerate the arm.

my bed was filled w/hands. i never know what tense we exist in. as the penicillin moves like sluggish fish through my system there is also him. the knowledge and sense of him who i adore. in this time where allah does not speak and where communing in tongue w/god can only result in death, i prefer the company and crave the existence of living gods. i examine the angel, roll it around my palm and smooth my finger against its parts. the image of a plate, marked charity, reels through the room into an amplifier and smashes. the floor is littered w/the bones of china. one of these pieces resembles an arm. i need a razor. my dress is damp w/mist and sweat.

when i got up i cut my feet. there was blood everywhere but i felt nothing. i needed a razor to slice through the atmosphere. i groped around through the fog, shut my eyes and ran my fingers up and down the arm of my angel. i felt the calloused hands and fell to my knees and kissed them a million times. he desires surrender, i surrender. i give him. his hands cradle and readjust my skull. i am crying but i am not happy. perhaps someone will cover my head w/the handkerchief. then properly adorned i can be led to the front lines of the procession to collide within the realm of an imagined accident.

robert bresson

i

i awoke w/new strength.

les enfants terribles was on the screen. since my ill-
ness i have installed in my sight a small screen and
projection booth. there are three films running con-
tinuously—terrible children, mademoiselle and
thomas the imposter. all blond films. for a while
there was only one film—au hazard balthazar. i saw
it several hundred times under mild sedation. for a
time my mind was a notebook of stills, annotations
and the art of this century.

specific, black and white. the enamel on canvas of
pollock. we are all children of jackson pollock. we
are all chaotic mutants—an extension of his action.
from his mad wrist spun us. just as we manifested
our own assault upon hymn via the vocal chords and
kind of little richard and james brown or mick jag-
ger. just as we cheated within dance, a discipline of
ritual abandon. just as we thrust on our own and
became one w/an arm going down on the sonic setup
of an electric guitar. i dream a lot of brancusi when
i play guitar. his struggle w/marble is my drama
w/rock. i like the feel of the neck. a strong solid
maple neck like the arm of a thick veined boy or the
throat of a conqueror.

ii

there is a close-up of marie. this is the same marie of
one-plus-one. the virgin guerilla gazes downward.
like the siennese madonnas she is able to hold a con-

versation w/the vein in her neck. she is the artist's model—eve the manipulable. she is the victim—the sacrificial lamb of inspiration.

gerard's hand is on her neck. his hands, like his clothes, are covered w/the extract of action-oil. like the artist he is what he does. his clothes are black because he is a poet. black is the uniform, the skin of poets. his clothes are black and so is oil—his medium. w/it he can abstract language into the physical hieroglyphics of convergence, of blue poles. art is work. work is a conscious act. art is a conscious act requiring the harnessing of the subconscious, nuclear energy and the discipline of the spirit. to create and to also create distance. then there is the inventor—the miracle of the telephone wire—the power corridors of detroit. where there is electric power there is violence. electric violence is man at his highest. marie is in the process of birth. gerard is swallowing lugers shaped like candies.

gerard equates painting w/a car skidding, crashing and sputtering. like no: 11, 14 this is no accident. the final icon is blueprinted behind his eyes. he knows what he wants to see and controls destruction. he pours oil over the road. he waits in the open field, his hands on his hips, laughing. one boy blends into another. his motorcycle, displaying the colors of maries tattered dress, lies on its side. he waits. he wants to feel what it tastes like to view the destruction of his creation in the process of ultimate completion. his expectations (fire, murder) are limitless. he harbors no potential remorse. he is a monster no less considerate than his brothers:

—de-kooning: decomposer of women
—gorky: illuminated coward
—rothko: black truth
—pollock: licensed killer

he also desires to witness his own immediate reaction to his creation and gradually the reaction of others. the reaction of the woman discovering her bleeding husband is a work of art. gerard is the creator but there are subcreators. a photographer raises his pentax and shoots her face. one shot follows another. the first shot was magic, a stolen moment. fresh grief is snowballed by test shots . . . into tri-x carcasse of sorrow.

the daughter wanders senseless into the field. the boy pulls her down w/him and forces her knees open. she is unable to speak or cry out. she is on the verge of phasing totally. he fucks her into awareness. when he feels the cry, gurgling and making its way up her throat, he silences it by jamming the chain from his bike between her teeth. now he is going to fuck her slow. he is going to witness her submission while her father is dying. as she spasms, her hand clutches the grass and clover. the hand of her father slips and

ceases its grip. here is another great work. her will and action are acting independently. here she is a criminal. a victim gives in; she is a participant. she is actively participating in her own glorious rape and the pathetic silent death of her father. she is no longer innocent but a living breathing work of art.

gerard is at work. all these details, his merging with woman, his destruction of man and nature, all are necessary components. the parts which will make up a total picture and the only true portrait of jackson pollock—coward, murderer and slob. a master pissing on the arched curls of villon. a master monster whose work resembled an arranged composite

of the days and nights of bungling. a frenchman is the first to recognize him. jackson pollock—the first true american artist wrestling with a totally american dilemma.

his death and his blood and the blood of bunny was his finest work. it spattered and shot like the first breath of a gusher. gerard thinks of these things as he is being shackled. he is being led to prison. his gesture says no. if a criminal is a failed artist then he is no criminal. look around. the girl, limp and gone, kisses his feet. over there, in the road, the door of the car merges permanently with the face of the deceased. the red light circles the weeping woman. the highway is littered with flash cubes and greasy debris. this is my finest work he tells them. i did this with my eyes open and my conscience naked and light. the man with the pentax will receive an award from the press for the woman's scream. what will i receive and why do you crucify me?

they chain him to a tree. he rubs his chin against the bark. then his cheek and mouth. he opens his lips and shoots his tongue in-and-out, hard-and-fast like a jet of healing seltzer. he presses against the tree. he is thinking of the girl and her violet neck. he is spurting in his pants, through his pants, onto the tree, into the limbs of life right there at the scene of action while they question him.

there is oil on the road.
this oil is the cause of the car going out of control. what we want to find out is who put the oil there and what the motive was.

who put the oil there?
i did.
motive
art.

i had to re-create the death of jackson pollock
w/the same radical destiny that spun from the
hallowed designs of his own death.
image: no. 11, 14 and portrait of a dream
image: the woman, lee krasner, shading her eyes
with hands brown and spotted.
here we have no accident no crime but a lateral
translation of a man going out of control
the initiation of a girl
who would teach
as her teacher
taught her.
axle grease
film of sorrow
who put this oil here?
i did.
motive
art.
who was your teacher?
robert bresson

burning roses

Father I am burning roses
father only God shall know
what the secret heart discloses
the ancient dances with the doe

Father I have sorely wounded
father I shall wound no more
I have waltzed among the thorns
where roses burn upon the floor

Daughter may you turn in laughter
a candle dreams a candle draws
the heart that burns
shall burn thereafter
may you turn as roses fall

thread

being away from you i have to feel you like some people feel god. projection from and to and in time. to spread around from the center of the son of mergence; the eye the essence of the eternal flame.

we connect and rush easily thru love and death. our kernel is hard and blessed. the foundation of the smooth barracks. i pass from house to hospital to void. it's my circulatory system. it's my rare and exquisite fortune of torture.

i was sitting by the window holding your button. i wanted to sew it on your coat but i was out of thread. it was dark and rainy and the leaves were shiny. i decided to go out and gather some up in my skirt for our carpet. i wanted to work on the hand of a soldier folded in prayer but i was out of thread. i remembered that there was a roll of silk in a box somewhere. you had given it to me when we were learning language. we shared words as treasure hunters joyfully uniting to piece together a tremendous stroke of luck. it was already there to be found. i unwound the bolt and felt a certain vibe a word. the word was the missing name of god. the word was written in your percussive blood.

a fleet of deer

a year has passed. i know this because there are that many more lines in my hand. in the center of my palm is a spiral. if i stare at it long enough it starts spinning. i have not seen him nor has he called on me in any form. i go through the motions of each day living a brighter richer life in dreams. i am used to a parallel existence. i am no stranger to the twenty-four track. but lately. lately i feel the night. the weight. i can't concentrate. i take a walk along the river. i stop to rest and watch my reflection ripple and crackle and beam. but it is not my face. the other night i lay back and felt his face consume and reshape my own. i couldn't move, gravity was dense and in debt upon me.

the luxury of sleep, rare moments of intense involvement with the present through labor or pleasure or a phone call from a friend. the uncovering of a certain memory. i turned and he was there, waiting, on his motorcycle. the shock of seeing him as i see him—an angel—quick, silent and corporeal in the banal setting of cars, whores and danglers made me dizzy with jealousy. i opened my eyes. the milky slant of his eyes, lidless and blue and gone.

ii

i rummage through the closet. it takes a long time, but i finally find what i'm looking for. a sack of red skin. inside are the remains of my fortune: a jacket, a pipe and a heavy blue button. i recognize the button. it's from his blue coat. as real in my hand as a

spoon or a guitar pick. it takes on the identity of
flesh. i grip my pipe. a lion carved from white clay.
pure and soft, hewn from the bottom of the mediter-
ranean sea w/a stem of amber. amber for good
health. the lion for gentle rule. it feels great in my
hands, like the essence of a guitar. hard yet yield-
ing. i have a long smoke within the confines of the
huge double closet. i lean my head against the mir-
rored door and prop my feet on the door opposite.
another mirror. in this way i can watch myself
smoke. i can watch myself fall apart or simply disap-
pear without care. i am a surgeon. the vigil of
tongue and scalpel. i am able to dissect the warped
and flowering mounds which make up my personal-
ities. i am able to do almost anything but free myself
from his eyes. from his ancient and sorrowful gaze.

as for my own eyes, i am unable to focus on any-
thing. like a lizard i am disgraced with the stigma of
two ways of watching. god i'm shot. i'm really tired.
i look at myself with my left eye. here i am victim-
maiden in prayer before illusion. here is discretion
and forgiveness. on the right plane is a blue and
bulging ball burning with the missive urge for im-
mediate frontal attack. i detest everything weak. i
am the military. i am the black poet in the cell fast-
ing and laughing. there is no fear that i will hang
myself here. it is well known that my scarf is re-
served as a vestment of vanity.

i understand genet because i am his brother. i am
weak and the exploiter of the weak. in life too i am a
prisoner. free to act and freeze and kneel and enact
my part in the smooth social order. in the play of life.

all the world is a stage because we relate shell to shell. we relate by chewing fat wads of sweet gum, blowing legend bubbles and feasting on the words within. words scribed by the master cartoonist. all our gestures and rhythums fit in the pattern of social rule like the bits of glass shaping the harmony within the kaleidoscope.

but what if one rebelled? one jagged edge pulling itself from the mire of melody up into the tube and choosing to scrape and puncture the open eye of a predictable merger. what if one refused and another and still another one until we all came to grips with this wonder of true love? of rock and roll? there is nothing but dream. nothing save the real truce with light. the flash and flood light on the root of the true interior. life is a dream? life is life. dream on the other hand is somewhere else. the state of purity on which we have once collided. that space has alluded us. rare moments and sex, often self inflicted, through work or illuminated nightmare but seldom with another. seldom do the two eyes meet. seldom is brother revealed as brother or a vision as vision. in life on this planet.

iii

i shut my eyes. when i open them i am on the summit of a valley of pure gold. there is no glare. for the gold is dull and powder like the hair of death as she goes running through the forest traced by a fleet of deer. in the clearing they are grazing, devouring flowers. their slender necks laced with amharic tattoo.

i am reckless. i never do anything according to the rules. there is a kink in me as regulated as the clock on the stove. when i go in to inspect time i stop and lean against the sink. i dig my heels deep into the flesh of the linoleum or the crude mosaics adorning the floor of the arena of the bull. the bull. a huge, black and shining specimen. the handle of crete.

his hard hump accommodates the acrobat. the head of a pin becomes eye of spider. i have been deprived of communicating in english. i am the eye of the eagle circling the arena of life. i am the eye, liquid and sour, poked and sucked from the curious bird. trembling to express the inexpressible. filled with the objective lust of the archeologist. i crave discipline, self contradiction. i am incapable of plot. skin graph perhaps but not plot. we pray to break our fear of submission to sensation. to strap within the movement of the roller coaster. to give in. exhale. to scream. to offer up oneself to the sacred bull charging and tearing into the skirts of repression. to lift ourselves up to the greedy assault of the stranger. i would do it all. rape, morte. give in totally to the rhythum of his whims all for the rush of unveiling and comprehending just one letter of the ancient alphabet.

scream of the butterfly

reflections on an american prayer jim morrison (electra)

i

(the dream)

The man, a changeling, journeys across the radiant waste of the American west. there is a quake, a crack. he sprawls. he laughs. he sticks his prick into the jagged warp and spews his seed thru the hard red vein of the desert. he does not emerge. he cannot rise. he is caught in the mouth of the wilderness. gestures of sound but no sound. there is to be silence before God.

But he is not silent. this time the gestures explode into music. into violence. he will not settle into a blissful jam. he is not occidental. he is the twisting remains of these united states. he desires not peace, but a piece of. he will not zip up, be good, shut up. he wants a bite. a slice of yet another life.

Tell them james, how we pray screaming.

Tell them jim, of the burden of mutation.

In the back of his mind, a crown of thorns spins and lands on the head of another. the ageless perfect center.

Jim Morrison was an artist. a member of the rude order of celestial screamers. one who would slaughter his brother to waggle tongues with his father: the absolute kiss and caress of death. the artist embraces his creator.

Ultimate incest.

ii

(should we eat this document)

A messenger appears. A cassette in plain envelope. No information. No clue as to packaging. We take it on the road. For several days we cannot even look at it. Holiday Inn. Dawn. We take it out and put it on. We put it on 'cause it serves as a gun to aim and fire more than a few true holes in the dismal machine that man still calls radio.

The reasons for resisting it were good clean reasons. The instinct to protect the vulnerability of the artist. The respect for his privacy and most of all his conceit. There's something slightly sacrilegious about viewing an artist thru the hands of others. Like strings over Hank Williams. Like the corpse postmortician.

But the aura of Jim Morrison is strong enough to armor his work against excessive doctoring. And *An American Prayer* has been pieced together delicately with obsessive devotion. Its flaws lie in the forgivable limitations of these friends and sometimes in the poet himself. For, like Sterling Hayden, he is the possessor of a strange sense of timing.

Some of it is regional. The California beatnik stuff
. . . the weird way L.A. people dance. But at best he is
a west coast Walt Whitman. A square that com-
munes with the gods.

In biblical times he may have appeared as Moses
or Samson or his pick of mad prophets. Today the
drama of his intensity seems dated. Dated in its pas-
sion and innocence, like *West Side Story* or *The
Grapes of Wrath*. But he was always dated, at his
most literal, even, when he was around. Bigger than
life and so he was laughable. Laughed at by the
court but loved by the people.

He possessed as a weapon this love and a remark-
able sense of humor. A nigger out of step with the
latest dance, who could suddenly turn and deliver a
line like "we could plan a murder or start a religion."

His fatal flaw was that his most precious skin was
the thin membrane that housed the blood of the poet.
He pledged his allegiance, in the end, to language.
And it did him in. Made an expatriot of him. As the
word, like him, is obsolete in our time on our radio.

And what will be done with him, his prayer?
Where does a guy like him fit in? He stood on a tradi-
tion of men who could not be bought. Men that disin-
tegrated fast, when borrowed, like salt in the rain.

As his friends sought to piece him together so the
people must preserve him. It is worth the effort to
fight for the rights of our generation's most vigor-
ous and aggressive poet.

An American Prayer documents a fragment of the
passion of Jim Morrison. It is not art as he would
have it, but nothing posthumous is perfect. It is not
the whole picture but the best part of the trip is in-
tact. And like finding a roll of Diego Rivera's under

an industrial sink, it is treasure unearthed. We feel
a sense of guilt but we are grateful for the glimpse.
Notes toward a symphony of ritual. Last movements
to reach out, to penetrate. New information. New
ammunition and that is truly something.

Enough to base a movie on. Tho I do regret that I
will not be called upon to play the part of the actor
out on loan.

iii
(the future looks . . .)

A child is a flower
His head is just floating in the
breeze.

—Jim Morrison

The artist is blessed with the curse of unceasing
labor, we slip our hands beneath the birth of his
work. we hide in the rushes. we build a raft. work
sails away.

The artist must not be stopped. his cries are not to
be censored, altered or suppressed. he serves the
middle ages, the final century, the sucking cosmos.
his is the irritant, a tear to slaughter, caught like a
wing in the palm of the hand and stretching across
the plain like a bloody western sunset.

An American Prayer resounds in the silence that
surrounds the cocoon of the lord. he is sleeping.
hibernating. awaiting the changeling and the ele-
gance of his change.

Y

Y is the covenant
between the artist
and the creator

Y is Yaweh
the name/the hands
that rearrange

Y is the palm
the rod the river
a system of law
that shall not
be mastered

Y is the trinity
the body
the shaft
the shadow cast

Y is the way of youth
the piss of sentinels
the forgotten vowel

Y is still life
the last shot
before death
a floating gardenia
a storm under glass
a motion of tulips
the hybrid the source

Y is the exhausted
inexhaustible force

combe

already i am at the end.
is it not strange that i should splay foot
a path so twisted and gridded. over broken
glass and caustic net. here i stalk. a wild
and alien indian. here I scoot through the
brush into the area of amalgamated breeding.
to the right an atomic energy plant surrounded
on all sides by an electric fence. over the
entrance is a sign not yet ciphered. it
could mean victory. it could mean danger.

i am in favor of these united states, here is
a land baptised and broken. here are the rising
foundations for the spartan existence. the family
will no longer control the western hemisphere. it
will exist in its pleasure but not in its tyranny.
our lungs will extoll the notes of a pure, more
powerful democracy intricate in its simplistics.
a leadership of snowflakes.

we are the adrenal people. we risk our lives.
we give birth to the word. a natural gamble
in the hand of code.
code is law and code is love.
a body of thought that houses illumination.
formed of the limb and the trunk of the tree.
from its branches the children swing. beneath
its shadows they stretch their arms and gaze
into the sky. something white is falling. cold
clean and welcome. some catch it on their tongue.
others create small weapons. still others stand,
immobile, as it falls veiling their locks.

at the end of the road the people work. cleaning
and straightening wood. carving and adorning the
canoes which will slide the waters. sleek silver
bullets racing the surface black and revelling
as the future on a flickering video screen.

we feed the distances. we salute one another.
we are the adrenal people. as children we were
graced with the gift of dematerialization. we
were also able to construct the scenes of great
mysteries. on the tip of each spinal tongue was
a pearl. the bait and calcium of the object was
discarded. the word pearl, however, was venerated
and catalogued. flora, fauna, emotion and mineral
all inspiration for the creation of a name—a word.

something white fell from the sky. we whirled
beneath it. we adored we named it. everything
was new to us and each artifact—every leaf was
carefully termed and examined like the rump of
a fresh cadet. the ribs of the venetian kept us
amused and pounding for several hours. and the
sun. we nearly cried for the sight of it.

i am on the path winding away. a tower. a toy.
a butterfly. everything is absurd, delightful.
but the greatest thing of all is the book.
are the cryptic tablets—the tombstones of
sculptors. there is no existing translation.

i am on the path. just another alien indian.
a being pushed by a higher hand. higher than
adrenalin higher than the tree.

do you believe in god?
he is my trainer.
the shadow that boxed me. the trainer that
jesters me on. we have entered a new period
of gain. a new state of time. we are here and
joyful to be so. here there is choice—a system
of action or action random and terrible.

to reinvolve ourselves we must face the past
with the existing spirit of the future, each
day i awake and a comb is lying on the pillow.
it is not mine. it belongs to my ancestor. it
belongs to a time experienced by the old city.

the comb i press to my scalp. i feel it
relates to the skull of the soul but its
function is not coming in.
a coronet of stars
ornament of the tame
no one to bow to
to vow to
to blame
how did i die?
i tried to walk thru light
with tangled hair
not yet prepared
for the valley of combat

wave
To Albino Luciano

hi, hi, I was running after you for a long time.
I like to watch you when you're walking
back and forth on the beach
and the way your cloth looks
I like to see the edges get all wet
when you're walking near the water there.
it's real nice to talk to you
I saw you from your balcony window
and you were standing there waving to everybody.
it was really great because there was about
a billion people but when I was waving
the way your face was it made me feel like you
it's not that you were just waving to me but
that we were waving to each other
it was really wonderful
it really made me feel happy
and um i.i.i. just wanted to thank you
because
you
you made me
feel good
oh

oh, it's nothing
well i'm just clumsy
no, it's just a bandaid.
no. it's ok.
oh no, something's always
happening to me
yeah, well i'll be seeing
ya

goodbye
wave
goodbye sir
goodbye papa

wave thou art pretty
wave thou art high
wave to the city
wave to the sky

wave thou art future
wave thou art why
wave to the children
wave wave goodbye

patti smith group   salutes

pope jean paul I

florence

She greeted us with open arms but I hardly noticed. Too steeped in where we'd been to see where we were going. Last night it was Bologna. We entered the perimeters of the arena and were flanked by soldiers. Younger than us maybe but armed with machine guns. My brother came for us. He looked pale but he never said a word. He motioned with us with a flashlight just like always and there they were guns poised. Not one smile not a word of explanation. This I felt called for action. Some kind of christian retaliation. And flanked by uniform I stopped suddenly and dropped to my knees and offered a prayer. The musicians stopped as well and held their ground. My brother stood with that look—"ready to die" it said.

Machine guns in Bologna Alfa Milano Armani Ferrari the Roman rain. I pulled my watch cap over my ears. The bus was rounding the hills. Transisters blaring colliding into the same song. rainy day women . . . peace train . . . the dreams dream . . . Gazing out the window battling motion sickness. A woman flags us down. They threw her husband in jail. They slapped red paint across her dress. Richard comforts her. My brother holds his station. Another flag. The drunken poet boards. The Rose of Sharon with trousers tied with twisted vine. He paces the aisle demanding money; spouting beauty, obscenities.

I look up at the sky. I imagine the pope descending upon us Fellini style. Atop a helicopter like Jesus

Sao Paulo his white arms outstretched. He waves his holy wand. Children, what do you wish for? The poet wants a suit of white linen lined with lire. The musician wants redemption. The boys want the girls to abandon their crosses and run away with them for one afternoon into a field tinged with gold. The woman wants her husband, vengeance. She grips my ankle. I am not Fidelio, I breathe. The pope wipes her distracted tears. No wish refused my dear.

And you, he looks at me, seeing thru my military air. What do you want. I have thought about it. I guess I have always known. I reach within my coat and extract an envelope, Please sir, I want you to deliver this letter to Michelangelo. In the distant hills a beautiful mist.
In the distant hills . . .

ii
And now we depart those same hills. All has been accomplished. How tired I am. I pull my watch cap over my ears. Farewell Firenze, you are a jewel and long may live your facets. I have sung to your children. They descended upon us like waves; like wolves. They have torn my clothes and collected my hair scraps. They have trampled my boots. They no longer resemble me.
And that is as I wish.
What have we done?
We have reinvented frenzy.
I watch my brother and his crew break down the equipment. He kneels in the shadows with a cigarette dangling from his lip. Brother when you were six I rescued you from the enemy and you pledged allegiance. Now you are free and I realize that I shall

never again experience such selfless devotion, such singular care. He looks up, smiles and salutes.

iii

Cara Michelangelo,

I opened my window and looked down upon the little cafe where I had spent the afternoon. I meant to visit the Piazzo that houses your work but instead sat rooted at my table before a plate of truffle sandwiches drinking coffee all day long thinking . . .

I paced my room. 4 A.M. The Grand Hotel Minerva. Roman goddess of wisdom. Why did I feel that I knew nothing. I could not breathe. I threw open the shutters but the air was still. I had to get out and I did. From the street I looked up and saw my musicians, unable to sleep as well, pressing their hands against the glass.

I tried to get lost but you were with me. You would not be denied. I found myself in a famous square lit by the yellow moon. I saw two youths embrace beneath the watchful eye of David. The shock of seeing him—white, defiant altogether beautiful, forced me to my knees. I rose and advanced with my arms outstretched. Michelangelo, here is a head. We lay it before the feet of your creation. The head of devotion, freedom and all the disjointed thoughts within. Michelangelo, you were a slave. Of love, of God, of your own fearsome intelligence. a slave. Like all great men you were called and you answered with great works. You gave us the shepherd boy. The Pietà. The twisting soul of the slave.

You had the calling and died wondering—who is it that calls. We were all calling. Down from the centuries beseeching you to release from stone unparalleled beauty and in doing so chipping away the stone encasing hearts.

Like all great men you were called. And like the Greatest Man, you remembered us—the future. Like Him you considered our loneliness, our confusion, our strife.

We were calling you and I am calling you now. Hail sir! We salute you. Your struggle was not in vain. Your struggle lives on in the wriggling of a babe in the arms of a delirious man. In the limbs of a runner barely able to comprehend breath. And in the eyes of the weary one, rounding the hills, about to sleep.

last tour notes
italia september 1979

wing

I was the wing
the spirits send
I was the feather
yet now offend
I was the sail
a smile formed
wrapping the arms
of the comic one
I was the thrust
a happy shoulder
I was the grandeur
the angels offer
I was the wing
in heaven blue
yet to trod
in heavy shoes
a soldier foot
of mortal worth
bound to earth
bound to earth

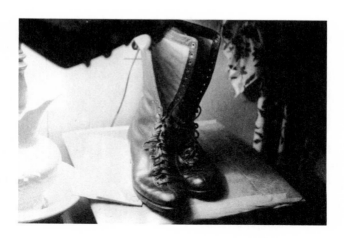

italy (the round)

for pasolini

picking thru the ruins with a stick. the wet leaves
against my legs and the bottoms of my feet. in my
pocket the silky roll of my stockings. my stomach is
contracting. the stones are cold and wet. the rein of
virgil and in the distance another castle, parted like
the scalp of a student, by a seizure of mold. the quaa-
ludes. the fluid muscle of the crowd. the hot lights.
action as a blade that cuts another slice. history.
limbs. nostalgic ruins in/ruin. the suspicious rivers
and the caves of naples. a ripple in the water is an-
other rib. floating dog. an anklet. a photograph-
posthumous blank. a still from a film not shot.

observe cinema! what is kinder more flattering than
images released with breath? a still? death frozen
and flat in a dimension of shadow and point. or the
final shots of pasolini mugging mineo in an alley.
emotion surfaces on the face or a screen. the light
projects thru the pores of a face of promise. phasing
future fusion. filling veins with ice until one is alto-
gether numb.

dubbed and brittle i can not speak. i am unable to
read my lines. the lights make my lids sweat and my
eyes fill with salt. i never saw so many tears. i seek a
way out. funeral music is not abstract. a dirge
evokes wailing and weight. the film/maker is
blinded by the bright night. he has gone under-
ground he has gone under. somewhere a slayer goes

undercover. fascist or lover it doesn't matter. the scenes of pasolini remain even as he is lowered. a flag of flies unfurl. over there, in the flowers, erect fellows playmate. their sticky plumage curdles the blood of observers.

the distress of molten cadavers. the winds shift and my nostrils split. the rigid triangle the bolt of the hare. now racing now clinging to the great wave. a bright green feel. molecules drop and accumulate in the shifting treasure box. the box tips and the molecules slip and slide down a ramp of sight rays. i am lying on my side within the bowels of a captive plane. the copilot is exploring the cockpit—my intestines. i am attempting to poke a finger thru the pale membrane of a window. to adorn with insertions a bank of corrosion. a wind screen of gyrating inlay. mercy god. my imagination is so dense i must machete. the jungle thick with breach of promise to sleep in peace. this potent state of grace is corrupted with the construction of amazing takes. photographs. stills from a scene not shot. messages. hands. the rows of silence. the rotating hips of our lady of the latin highway. dwelling in favor in the caves of italy.

the rocksound. i am ninety feet up. attached to each foot is the deck of a ship. the mast is becoming wings. hair ribbons. the night just laughs just roars. light splinters. i've been up here before on this hot walk. the alcohol is exotic and thick with sugar. contraband cigarettes and hot liquors. my fingers are melting but i no longer need them. in the distance—musings, rock is the amplification of the

lower head, so arranged that the whole inflores-
cence resounds as one blooming note.

OPERA IS TRUTH AND CARUSO IS QUEEN

a salon. a salad and cocaine as the seasoning. the
white and impulsive grain that lines the sacristal
and sexual throat.

the hotel de france. hard sailors from vienna. the
motorcycle scores. seams bursting in leather and
the aristocratic scams of the leather rider. all this
exists. woman is as prehistoric as a kiss. and here is
one shaking her palms at the sky. an actress of un-
measurable task shot by none save the eye of I.

the hot breath and false caresses of a fisherman dig-
ging a hook deep in the root of the neck of a heroine.
she is overcome. first with desire and then the desire
not to be snuffed out. flutter of hand and lids. seven
movements becoming seven stills in the archives of
the forbidden cinema. that which has no perceivable
direction. that which is not yet shot. the sleeve of a
silk robe rolled up. the burning cotton. alcohol. she
is shot up delicate, discreet. drifting in a cushion—
massive and functional as a cloud. the slanted posi-
tion of the maiden neo-pronto. the erect muscle, the
thrust of a hip glistening with crisco and sweat. the
beads strung together within strands of spittle.
freeze frame. the hand of the hero—the uranian
guerrilla. a minute 2-way radio. platinum antennae
dotted with eyes of sapphire. he runs his fingers
along the artiface. perforated jewels pock the
smooth surface of his aching palms.

he leaps. he is free and stumbling over the rocks, dehumanized by war. no ties with the shore, he drags thru the tired halls that lead to the grande ballroom. drawings of motion. he spins and collides into a wall of sound—breaking thru the spectacle of illusion. ladies levitate. robots with hearts of god serve and extend. the art of technology. the electric guitar is a voice as well as device. a bird in space. an oscar—sizzling sculpture yearning to be palmed.

a slow dissolve. my hands are burrowing filth. earth too, is alexander. i sup and plot and map out my territory—this earth i have been eating. i am strong and ready for the climb. i enter a ballroom littered with oversized film cans. shots are blown on the curve of an exit. there is no way out; we are alone together. he has the eyes and and clothes of combat. we are tracked within an expansive joke—a majestic budget—a love travelogue seen by none and lived by some. rapture 7. wherein the former spectators are now the stars caught in the universe of mutual and prophetic trance.

Regard! she is my face
Regard! slots everywhere
—the music is visceral
—poem as plot
—a poem is a collection of words and mixed grill
a powerful sequence: a grey mule ejaculating and a young girl splitting. underexposure. it is impossible to identify or deface her.

the ping of the xylophone is not rain. transcend violin. a roof of tears and corrogated tin. violence becomes them and he is purple and impatient and pummeling.

the films are disintegrating, amateur, breaking into
parts. the heroine removes herself from the fading
aura. in life, in lens, they embark. the drums sound.
—it's a ship
—no it's a motor
—no it's my heart
oxygen on my back. naked and greased. in black. my
heart beating like mad. moving thru the black box.
free of adornment. the wind screams thru the tiny
holes in my naked ears.

a flash vessel

print out

—note on immortality—

WITHOUT THAT INCONSIDERATE CUT
I COULD HAVE RULED THE WORLD—
WITHOUT THAT RUDE SLICE
THIS MOVIE WOULD HAVE GONE ON FOREVER—

the horns. the relentless sounding. i want to put on
wild is the wind. looking at you. i want to cut off all
my hair and take a drug and another drug. love.
monocaine. peel away my layers, skin after skin, of
translucent film.

italy. how lovely you are. and how treacherous is
your makeup. i am an insect, a movie star. where are
my shades and my boots i am lost. i have taken a lot
of speed and i can't bear to live outside film. the radio
and the waves of the sea. i'm coming down i'm
throwing up. the radio says they are burning the
fields. the blood of the poppies. the metallic mouth of
a woman sleeping.

the actress blows kisses to pierre pa-olo rising from
the sea. victim of fascists and faggots and the purity
of his art. waving goodbye. the thrust of his arm. the
trust of his view.

pasolini is dead. et morte. shower of petals. flower
girls deflowered. virgins skewered and devoured.
film-deaths of hollywood stars runs simultaneous
split screen 24 hours. vats of flesh and grape shot
thru amo valves of cannons. balls of sight. falconetti
advancing in a suit of turquoise armor. a tuxedo of
manner. on the long beach twist men with scales of
sores for wings excreting chalone. ocean spittle and
slobbering heart. picking the ruins—our pates with
a stick. our mines are going. we bleed on the sheets.
diamonds, not coal, cease to exist. fuel lives! and life,
like film, goes on.

true music

Time is expressed
in the heart
of an instrument
Something that stops
in the heart of a man
Time is the wall and the space around
Time is the tree a life that resounds
Time to adore and time to go
To give to the fisherman
the slippers of Rome
the whirling embrace
the arms of the fold
to gather together
the swirl of the leaves
turning and falling
returning as thee
to the clay of creation
tho' your children will hold
the wave of your hand
the smile of your soul

I wish to express my appreciation
to my husband, my love and guide

to Andreas Brown for proposing this project
to my editor Amy Cherry
to Bill Rusin, Patricia Anthonyson, Nancy Palmquist,
Leslie Sharpe, and all at W. W. Norton
to all at Hanuman Books
to the Estate of Robert Mapplethorpe
to Lenny Kaye and Andi Ostrowe for gathering
and transcribing unpublished material
to Jane Friedman and William Targ and all who first
encouraged me to write and continue writing.

acknowledgments